STRATEGIC DATABASE MARKETING

Rob Jackson
Vice President
Marketing & Information Services
Donnelley Marketing Inc.

Paul Wang Ph.D.
Integrated Marketing Communications
Medill School of Journalism
Northwestern University

Foreword by Don E. Schultz

NTC Business Books
a division of *NTC Publishing Group* • Lincolnwood, Illinois USA

Library of Congress Cataloging-in-Publication Data

Jackson, Robert R.
    Strategic database marketing / Robert R. Jackson, Paul Wang.
       p.   cm.
    Includes bibliographical references and index.
    ISBN 0–8442–3232–7
    1. Database marketing.   I. Wang, Paul. II. Title. III. Title:
Strategic database marketing.
HF5415.126.J33 1994
658.8'4—dc20   93–42154
                                               CIP

Published by NTC Business Books, a division of NTC Publishing Group
4255 West Touhy Avenue, Lincolnwood (Chicago), Illinois 60646-1975, U.S.A.
© 1994 by NTC Publishing Group.
Manufactured in the United States of America.

4 5 6 7 8 9 ML 9 8 7 6 5 4 3 2 1

DEDICATION

This book started almost five years ago, as the seed of an idea on how to present database marketing in terms of a methodology. It has been quite an adventure and effort to complete. There are too many friends and fellow database marketers who have offered us encouragement and expertise, and have stuck with us from the beginning to list here. To all of you, please accept our thanks! Special mention goes to Don Schultz who urged us on from the beginning, to NTC Publishing Group for keeping the faith, and to Lisa Petrison for her help with the writing of the book.

To Ruth, who has encouraged me and believed in me through this labor of love, and to my son Robert, a future database marketer.

Rob Jackson

To Lisa, whose continuous support has kept me going through this long project.

Paul Wang

C O N T E N T S

F O R E W O R D

Don E. Schultz, Ph D
Northwestern University
President, Agora, Inc.

In the late 1980s, when the editors of NTC Business Books approached me to recommend an author for a book on database marketing, there was no hesitancy on my part. "Get Rob Jackson and Paul Wang together," I said. "You'll have the best of both worlds." Rob, the practitioner, who takes a thoroughly grounded, sometimes almost academic approach to database marketing. And, Paul, the pragmatic academician, who thinks and acts like a practitioner. The book before you is the result. I think you will agree the combination not only worked but it has set a new direction for database marketing.

The title really tells the story, *Strategic Database Marketing.* It is strategic. It tells managers what they need to know. It takes the long-term view, the business-based approach to database marketing. It tells you what database marketing will mean to your business, plus the *why* and the *how* of putting a database system into action. This is a rather dramatic change from other books available. Strategies. Not more tactics, although there are plenty of examples to illustrate the points. Not more "how to," for today the major questions are *why* and *with what results.* Not more illustrations of layouts and flow charts. Yes, you will find those included, for they are necessary to illustrate how successful companies are making database marketing work. But, they are there not to impress or overwhelm, but to explain. And, you will not find a maze of technical jargon with lambdas and gammas and summation signs. Granted, you might find a few just to assure you that what you are reading is well grounded in theory. Instead, what you will find is a clearly written, direct, managerial approach to database marketing. No smoke. No mirrors. No hyperbole. No inviting, but unfilled, promises. Jackson and Wang have too much experience for that. They know what works, for they have been there, from the beginning. And, they continue to be on the forefront of database marketing thought and training. That is what makes *Strategic Database Marketing* unique in the field.

Why is this book so special to me? Having edited the *Journal of Direct Marketing* since its inception, I have seen database and direct marketing, and all the other allied fields, grow and mature. This is the first book that puts database marketing where it belongs, at the center of all marketing activity. When Jackson and Wang introduce their "Three Points of Entry into Database Marketing," their first statement tells the whole story: "An organization's technical database solution should be designed around its marketing requirements." Database and marketing. Intertwined and intermixed. Not separate units. Not different functions. Integrated. Strategic. Managerial. That is the tone and the substance of the entire book.

A major concern for organizations considering database marketing is finding out who, beyond the traditional direct marketing and catalog organizations, can or is doing database marketing and doing it well. Jackson and Wang draw on their broad industry and consulting experiences to illustrate how database marketing can work through the use of nine case histories in just one chapter. These range from a major package goods company to a Nevada hotel and casino. Although the companies have been disguised, each illustrates how database marketing can and has been used to change and build any type of business. Strategic. Managerial.

A key part of any discussion of database marketing is the technology that drives it. Here, you will find a comprehensible and realistic discussion of technology, honed and refined on the direct and database marketing lecture and conference circuit. This is technology for the manager, not the "technonerd." Jackson and Wang provide a clear, concise, managerial discussion of files, storage, platforms, and software that will allow you to intelligently determine and discuss what you, as a manager, need in a system or process.

Most importantly, Jackson and Wang put database marketing in its proper place in the marketing hierarchy, as the new way to really "do" marketing. Not an add-on. Not a technical step forward. Instead database is viewed as a truly revolutionary change in marketing practices that will take us into the 21st century.

For years, all of us, myself included, have preached the marketing concept— that is, be customer focused. Developing customers, not products. Retaining consumers, not constant conquest of new prospects. But, in my experience, only a few organizations have been able to practice that approach. Database marketing now provides the system and process for all organizations to really become "marketing organizations." Much of this new database approach to marketing is based on the concept of lifetime value. Lifetime value in the way and manner that *all* organizations can practice it, not just the traditional catalog or direct marketer.

As is true in life, and in most database experiences, all is not sweetness and light in the land of technology and bytes and RAMs and ROMs. Two of the critical ingredients in making database marketing work are: (a) getting top management approval for the investment and on-going cost, and (b) getting organizational acceptance and support for a new way of doing marketing. Both subjects are treated in detail. And, both from a managerial view. No hype. No magic formulas. Just solid, industry-based experience from a couple of guys who have helped build a number of businesses successfully.

Finally, there are social implications of database marketing. While as marketers we know what we can do with the technology, the question is: What will consumers and regulators let us do in the future? Managing the expectations and realities of database marketing begs the important social issues of privacy and environmental waste. To ignore these major questions is to ignore the future of database marketing. For database marketing will only grow and mature if consumers and customers agree it is a good thing. Something that is beneficial to both parties, not just one. Consumer driven. Consumer responsive. Consumer dependent. Consumer controlled. That is database marketing of the future.

Will you enjoy this book? If you have ever seen Jackson and Wang at one of their many appearances before direct and database marketing groups, you know you are in for a treat. It is like a seminar, symposium, and discussion in print. It is database marketing as it is and as it should be. It is database marketing for the manager. It is strategic database marketing. Read on.

INTRODUCTION

If you spend much time around small children, you've probably had occasion to read and read and read again many fairy tales and fables. One that you will remember is *The Tortoise and the Hare.* The moral for a three-year-old, of course, is that slow and steady wins the race. But, as we think about this advice and the business world, there is only one response—nonsense!

In today's business world, slow and steady does not necessarily mean success. In fact, a slow and steady tortoise will most likely be left far behind by a focused, aggressive hare. Marketers must be willing to change as new techniques come along that can move their businesses forward. And there is only one way to beat the competition at its own game—through sales!

Sales and revenue are the goal of any commercial enterprise . . . they always have been and always will be. Sell more and make more money.

This book is about sales, but it is also about creating customers. This raises an interesting question for a future generation of marketers. Which is more important, making a sale or creating a customer? We believe, without any doubt, that creating a customer is the key to success. Once you have a customer, you have a first sale *and* an opportunity to make the second, third, and more sales over time. If you settle for a single sale but lose the customer, you must start over and resell each and every time.

Strategic Database Marketing is about creating customers. It will help you maximize sales by establishing and nurturing customer relationships. The tool we use to do this is the database. It is the means through which you can build a long-term, interactive relationship between your product, your service, or your business and your customers. Database technology is no mystic answer to marketing problems, but a tool that will allow any marketer to become a more efficient and effective communicator with customers and prospects.

In this book, we will create a framework for the understanding and development of a database-driven marketing communications program tailored to your business. We believe, and we hope that we can persuade you to believe, that a database can become a powerful resource for your business. One that will create and nurture customers . . . and increase sales and profits.

Part I of the book looks at the phenomenal changes in consumers and consumer behavior that have opened up tremendous opportunity in database marketing. At the same time, we see how huge leaps forward in technology have made such opportunities achievable.

In Part II we explain what database technology is and how it works. We describe the enormous range of applications through which marketers can create and develop long-term, profitable relationships with customers.

In Part III, we establish three basic "building blocks" for developing a database marketing system. Just as a child can build everything from simple boxes to elaborate castles out of toy blocks, marketers can build databases as simple or as sophisticated as their changing needs dictate. We identify the three key ingredients of a database program as:

1. Data,

2. Technology, and

3. Statistical techniques.

As you read, you will learn how they can work together to improve your business.

Part IV provides guidelines for getting your own customized database marketing up and running and for managing it effectively. We explain how to develop database marketing strategies in tune with overall business objectives and how to sell the database program to top management and prove that it will bring in a substantial return on investment.

Part V addresses issues that will affect future advances in database marketing, and explains how to keep your system current and competitive.

The Great Database Marketing Paradox

Before you go on with your quest to develop a marketing database, we would like to give you the benefit of a trend we have observed among organizations setting up systems for the first time. We call it the Great Database Marketing Paradox.

At the outset of developing the marketing database, companies make major financial and resource commitments. The result is a database of customers and/or prospects that meets initial expectations.

Once the system is set up, however, the expectations and the reality of database marketing begin to drift apart. Companies neglect to factor in the continuing cost of maintaining the database—keeping up with newer technology, applying research and segmentation techniques, collecting new and more sophisticated customer information, and so on. After all, a database is only as powerful as the data it holds and the research techniques that allow you to access it. There are too many case histories of organizations that have failed to anticipate, understand, or plan for the ongoing resources required to succeed in database marketing. As you read this book, realize that database marketing is a combination of strategic marketing planning, creative communications, data, technology, and statistical analysis techniques. All are critical for the success of your program. Do not get trapped with a database that will not meet expectations. Plan a system that provides all the resources necessary to successfully implement, maintain, and manage your database marketing program into the future.

I

What Has Happened to Marketing?

Why Marketing Needs Database Technology

Now, marketers of mass consumer products ranging from cars to coffee are turning from the TV box to the mailbox. Package goods companies . . . are relying more on targeted media.

Business Week, September 23, 1991

We hear over and over in the business press that today is the age of the individual. To be successful, we hear that marketers must focus on their customers as unique, all with different ambitions, perceptions, likes and needs. This "new" focus on the customer is really not so new at all. If you look back into our marketing past, attentiveness to the customer was the rule, not the exception. Started well before the industrial revolution, care of the customer still flourishes in small towns today and is practiced nationally by entrepreneurial retailers. It is also the trademark of a new breed of customer-oriented marketers.

The thread these marketers all have in common is that they *really* know their customers. Not just their names and addresses, but their family members, special interests, *and* their buying preferences.

Early small-town merchants remembered the products each customer purchased and made recommendations based on past purchases and lifestyles. Often, products were modified or custom-produced for their needs. The customer was king, and business was done on a handshake.

However, as time went by, we experienced a change in the dynamics of the customer/merchant relationship. Mass production led to volume buying and mass media advertising. The result was that marketers developed a different view of the customer. No longer unique, all customers were perceived to have the same needs and be reachable through the same channels with the same communications message. This was progress! Henry Ford could not have said it better, "We'll give you any color you want, as long as it's black."

3

Well, Henry, it is now clear to us that not everyone wants to buy black . . . or the new Coke either. In fact, convincing customers to buy your product or service has never been a more formidable task.

A Last Look at the Way Marketing Used to Be

We live in unique and fascinating times. Events in Eastern Europe and the former USSR are rewriting history faster than we can process and keep up with it. We are seeing history happen on our television screens night after night.

And changes in the business world keep pace with changes in our social, political, and cultural fabric. Changes in the media, distribution channels, competition, and myriad other factors have had dramatic and lasting impact on how marketers will communicate their products and services to customers for decades to come.

What used to be true for marketers is no longer so. We will put on our marketing historian hats for a few pages to show how the basic principles of marketing that just a few years ago guided us—the "used to be's" as we call them—no longer make sense. Their collapse has contributed to the steady and phenomenal growth of database marketing as a new way to get back in touch and to really communicate with our customers.

We will look at some new marketing truths that replace the "used to be's" that kept marketers at a distance from their customers.

Dick and Jane Are Not the Same!

Remember "Leave It to Beaver"? In the 1950s and 1960s this top TV show was a symbol of the good life. In fact, most people agreed on what the good life encompassed. "Leave It to Beaver" and the popular primer *Dick and Jane* told us of a life to which we should all aspire. Dick and Jane lived in a comfortable suburban house with their father (who held a job), their mother (who stayed at home), their little sister Baby Sally, and their dog . . . the famous Spot. Their home was tidy, the family was white, and you just knew that the parents owned that house and were paying off their mortgage just as fast as they could. Not everyone lived this lifestyle, but nearly everybody agreed that it was the ideal.

Today, fewer than seven percent of households fit the Dick-and-Jane profile. Modern families are split into many smaller segments . . . singles living alone or with roommates, married couples without children, unmarried couples living together, fathers or mothers heading households alone, homosexual couples, older "empty nesters," and many other permutations.

Even more important than the diversity of today's household, however, is the acceptance by society of that diversity. No longer is having children automatically thought better than being childless, or living in the suburbs better than living in the city, or being white better than being black or Hispanic or Asian. Our definition of what is acceptable has changed as the family has changed.

By the way, this same society now feels that chocolate, vanilla, and strawberry ice cream are not necessarily better than Baskin-Robbins' other 28 flavors, or Ford or Chevy better than other cars, or rock music better than jazz or apples better than kiwi fruit. We have become a society that acknowledges and accepts diversity. Dick and Jane are no longer the ideal.

While Dick and Jane's family was usually gathered around the television in the evening, it is quite a different story today. Leisure time has become one of the most precious commodities to today's consumer. And there are many more alternatives to television than there were even ten years ago. The demands of job and family have led consumers to make the most of their free time. They are embracing products such as microwave ovens, frozen gourmet dinners, and other time-savers that support their lifestyle changes.

Manufacturers have been forced to respond. Today, there are 752 different models of cars and trucks in the United States, more than 200 brands of cigarettes, and we will bet you cannot list all the variations of Coke or Pepsi in 30 seconds.

The point is that the dynamics of the consumer household have changed dramatically over the last several years. In an attempt to keep pace, manufacturers have diversified their product lines to match an increasingly diversified consumer base. Creating a vicious circle, it has then become increasingly difficult for any one brand to achieve significant market share, even with extensive marketing and promotion. The Dick and Jane era of one-size-fits-all mass marketing is over. It is now the age of niche marketing.

Good-bye GM

In a 1975 survey of male and female heads of households, 74 percent of the women and 80 percent of the men agreed with the statement, "I try to stick to well-known brand names." By 1984 only 58 percent of women and 52 percent of men agreed with the same statement. This trend has continued into the 1990s as retailers have developed their own brands. Consumers have become more likely to experiment with generics, store brands, or a prominently promoted price-off brand. They are also more likely to switch back and forth among major brands in a category.

The reasons for the decline of brand loyalty in general are hard to pinpoint. However, some things are clear. Consumers are less receptive to the constant bombardment of advertising messages for brands. And, as the brands struggle to hold share via price promotion techniques, consumers perceive less uniqueness and thus less value added to their standard brands. Added to this is a weakened economy where consumers pay more attention to purchases—if two leading brands in a category are similar, they will choose based on price.

According to *Business Week,* "Now, many Americans, brought up on a steady diet of commercials, view advertising with cynicism or indifference. With less money to shop, they're far more apt to buy on price. And, they're a lot less likely to be smitten by Tony the Tiger or the Campbell Kids." (*Business Week,* September 21, 1991.)

No category is more telling than cars. Imports have dramatically impacted sales of the "big three" manufacturers, GM, Ford, and Chrysler. GM, which had a 50 percent share of market in 1970, today has fallen to 35 percent. To the Dick and Jane family, GM could do no wrong. Why, GM was America. The best technology, engineering, manufacturing, and value anywhere. But GM did not react to the changing America. The imports did. Instead of the traditional technique of dictating style to consumers, international competitors developed cars to meet the changing lifestyle. Moreover, as image advertising became less effective, the big three turned to promotion to rev up sales and generate profits. Consumers learned that if you just waited 60 days, a new $1,500 rebate would come out.

For many consumers, shopping for discounts has become a leisure activity. Visit any urban area and you will find entire shopping malls dedicated to discount or outlet pricing. Practically any product that can be purchased at full price retail can also be found in discount or outlet stores. Consumers have become "deal shoppers," taking pride in finding products for 20, 40, 50 percent off or more.

The decline in brand loyalty whether shopping for cars, soap, cereal, or almost any other product can be attributed to a number of factors: excessive couponing and trade deals; deep price point promotions; the proliferation of brands, many of which seem the same to the consumer; consumer desire for variety; consumer education; and the economy. The bottom line for marketers is that there will be no consumer loyalty in the future unless it is earned and reinforced every time the consumer purchases the product. Good-bye to GM and any other giant that does not see the writing on the wall.

The Future Is Service

Today, you can take advantage of a wide variety of services that your parents never imagined. Services now generate 67 percent of the gross national product and employ seven out of every ten workers. Most meals today are eaten outside of the home; 40 percent of retail lawn-care product sales have been wiped out by the rise of lawn-care service companies; and consumers with the money but not the time can hire services to clean their houses, run their errands, walk their dogs, and wait for the furnace repair company to show up.

The rise of the service economy is at once the cause and the effect of consumers who have less and less time to spend on anything but the most pressing details of their lives. This increased time pressure is having a profound impact on consumers' buying behaviors—they are becoming more demanding, more impatient, and less likely to spend time agonizing over small purchases. The future is service, and service is—by definition—tailored to individual customer preferences.

Cable Me!

Twenty years ago, most Americans spent their evenings in front of the television set, watching network programming on NBC, CBS, or ABC. The cost of a 30- or 60-second commercial was within the budget of most major advertisers. Consumers also read newspapers and general-interest magazines such as *Life* and *Look*. Times have changed and mass media is experiencing a major downturn. Over the last several years, media revenue and spending has continued to decline and promotion expenditures have continued to increase steadily.

The reason is that today's busy consumers are unlikely to spend their evenings at home watching television. When they do, they are probably viewing from a cable system with options of 60 or more stations. They also rent videos or switch back and forth between stations with their remote controls. Meanwhile, the cost of network television advertising is rising to astronomical heights, and the cost of "covering all the bases" by adding spots on cable and local stations has become prohibitively expensive for most marketers. Similarly, consumers have stopped reading newspapers as frequently, and general-interest magazines have given way to a plethora of specialty publications that cater to a wide range of interests, but are more expensive for advertisers on a cost-per-thousand basis.

The trends are clear—mass media advertising will never be the same. The three networks are being hurt by cable, the possible emergence of a fourth or fifth additional network, syndicated television, and changing consumer lifestyles. While mass media will always play an important role in communicating the message of products and services, it will never again be the dominant resource it once was. According to *Business Week,* "Even if consumers remained staunchly brand loyal, marketers would be less willing to blanket them with media advertising. To be sure of reaching the right audience, companies once had no choice but to use general advertising campaigns, which reach nearly everybody. Now, computerized market research is letting them collect detailed information on their customers—not just the approximations offered by demographics, but the specifics of names and addresses." (*Business Week,* September 21, 1991.) As more and more consumers cry "cable me!," the picture becomes bleaker for mass marketers.

Gas and Hamburgers

Getting your product in front of the consumer is half the battle. However, this has become increasingly difficult for marketers today. Department stores are fighting for survival, and who would have figured that Wal-Mart and K Mart would overtake Sears in gross sales? The fight for shelf space and displays in supermarkets has become increasingly intense, and has forced many product categories (such as soft drinks and pet foods) to increase the use of trade deals to the point that very little product is purchased at full price.

Many brand marketers find themselves in a fight for survival with increasingly powerful retailers. Through micromarketing, retailers have taken control of their relationships with brand marketers. The trade controls the level and type of in-store promotions the brand can implement. The trade has also grown more sophisticated at developing its own customer communications programs, including multicoupon direct mail and relationship-oriented marketing programs. Manufacturers are afraid of becoming captive to retailers and of brands being marketed for the retailers' benefit rather than to build the brands' franchise or equity.

Personal selling is also less effective in all but a few categories, as most people are not home during the day and are afraid to answer their doors at night. In its place, who could have anticipated the addition of new distribution channels such as the continuing success of the Home Shopping Network and Quality Value Channel? Where does it all end? The answer is that business will continue to seek new and creative means of reaching the consumer. A recent experiment combining sales efforts to encourage customers to buy such diverse products as gasoline and fast food hamburgers *together* is just one example of marketers seeking to provide the consumer with convenience and time savings through double product distribution. This is a sign of the times.

Everyone—Even the Marketer—Is Accountable

Even in the heady days of mass marketing, accountability was a sore point. The impact on sales of mass media advertising has always been notoriously difficult to measure. "Sales increased when we advertised," marketers claimed, but hard evidence was lacking. Database technology can take this mystery out of communications programs—through precise tracking of sales, all communications can be accountable. Because of financial pressures that all companies face, brand marketing will as we move toward the year 2000 be required to prove that *all* communications efforts are reaching the mark, selling product, and increasing revenues.

What is the real impact of accountability on marketing? It used to be that marketers in a less competitive environment could count on and track significant growth in share of market or sales. However, today, with large brand categories, brand extensions, niche products, category maturity, and private labeling by retailers, most are happy just to maintain share.

For retailed brands or products, share, or per-customer sales, represents a subsegment of all available consumers. This usually equates to no more than 10 to 15 percent of all consumers, even for a dominant product. To reach consumers, marketers have in the past relied on three major tactics: mass media advertising, sales promotion, and in-store marketing.

Communicating with a hypothetical brand's 10 to 15 percent share of consumers through mass media advertising is wasteful, even in good times. The only factor that made it feasible in the past was low cost-per-thousand communication based upon the concept that everyone watched television. Moreover, the technology did not exist for marketers to isolate their 10 to 15 percent share of customers by name and address. Mass communication was the only choice. In today's marketing environment, this blanket approach no longer makes sense. Every week another obituary is written for network television. It is struggling with commercial-zapping, cable, VCRs, fragmentation with targeted programming, and commercial clutter. To make matters worse, according to some studies, up to 75 percent of television viewers cannot recall the advertisements they see.

In the new era of accountability, mass media advertising loses out. Though no other media is as powerful as television at creating and reinforcing brand equity, network television must be held to task for its failure to reach targeted audiences effectively and efficiently.

Sales promotion and in-store marketing, too, are under scrutiny. Most retail brands spend a large percentage of their marketing communications budget on sales promotion, primarily through delivering coupons via free-standing inserts (FSIs). All you have to do is open your Sunday newspaper to see how popular FSIs still are. However, FSIs offer little selective targeting potential, because everyone gets the same message and offer.

Redemption rates have decreased dramatically—by as much as 30 percent for some marketers over the last five years. At the same time, the face value of FSI coupons has increased by as much as 60 percent over the same five-year period. If this is not enough, the per-thousand cost to advertise via FSIs has increased each year. Dominant brands lock in calendar exclusivity, thus limiting availability. And misredemption rates cost marketers more and more each year.

The mass marketing tactics brands have come to rely on are simply no longer as effective as they once were. And the fact that they are not easily accountable makes them increasingly suspect. Manufacturers are under pressure to maintain growth and profits for stockholders. Marketing and brand management are trapped, forced to increase sales in the face of diminishing returns. It is no longer enough to say that "sales increased when we advertised." Management now wants proof of the ability of advertising to deliver results. Management is *demanding* accountability.

And accountability means more than a correlation between sales and communications. It is a measurement of the marketer's ability to persuade individuals to purchase or continue to purchase a product or service. Through the communications mix, sales must be won—one at a time—from current customers, from new customers, or from competitors' customers.

The difference is that it is no longer enough to understand customers and prospects by aggregate profiles. The battle for customers in the future will be won by marketers who understand how and why their customers *individually* buy their products—and who learn how to win them over, one customer at a time.

The bottom line is this: Marketers must be accountable, not for total sales, but for each and every customer. Marketing techniques that have worked so effectively in the past are better off left in the past.

Marketing Evolution and Revolution: Something Old Is New Again

Our focus on the new marketing truths or dynamics that replace the "used to be's" of marketing is an attempt to document changes in the marketplace. These changes are leading to a new way of thinking about how to communicate with the consumer. It is both an evolution and a revolution. Evolution in the respect that the demise of the "used to be's" has created permanent change in the marketing environment. Revolution because the merging of change and technology has created an opportunity for marketers to enter a new era of sophistication in understanding exactly who purchases their products. It also provides a means to communicate with customers based upon that knowledge. That merging of change and technology has resulted in the introduction of the customer database and the rise of database-driven marketing programs.

Our review of the marketing lessons of the past and the changes we face as marketers leads us to an unmistakable conclusion. If you view communications with the consumer along a continuum from the mass market to today's highly segmented niche markets, the focus is clearly on the individual. Rapp and Collins in their bestseller, *The Great Marketing Turnaround* (Prentice-Hall, 1990), describe the challenge: "It means rediscovering how to talk to individuals in a way that many in a new generation of marketers have never learned."

What is new is the need to focus our resources on the consumer as an individual. The fact that the "used to be's" are no longer true demonstrates that we have no choice. Our marketing environment has changed and there is no going back. Marketers must acquire, develop, and tap into a database of in-depth knowledge about their customers. The only way to communicate with them effectively is to use that knowledge. We must relearn a lesson from our recent past and make it the first commandment of our marketing future: "Know they customer and communicate with him or her based on what you know." A marketing database is the means through which we can do this.

C H A P T E R **2**

Information Is Power: How the Database Empowers Marketers

The law of the microcosm . . . Rather than pushing decisions up through the hierarchy, the power of microelectronics pulls them remorselessly down to the individual. This is the law of the microcosm. This is the secret of the new American challenge in the global economy.

George Gilder, *Microcosm*

We ended Chapter 1 with the new first commandment of marketing, "Know thy customer and communicate with him or her based on what you know." This principle represents the future of marketing, no matter what products or services you market. And it is the roadmap to success.

The concept of information, information management, and the database is not new. In fact, data processing solutions in information management have been used for applications such as finance, manufacturing, and human resources for years. Business could not survive if it could not manage massive amounts of data effectively and turn it into valuable information.

So why is database marketing considered such a new, hot topic? We blame it on the old "if it's not broken, don't fix it" mentality. And as we saw in the last chapter, it has taken about 20 years, but finally, marketers are admitting that the mass market is, indeed, broken beyond repair. What is new is the emergence of database technology, applications that allow marketers to tap into real information about their customers and prospects. According to *Business Week* (September 23, 1991), "At the same time consumers have changed, technology and the proliferation of media are transforming the science of marketing to them. Now, companies increasingly can aim their messages to carefully pinpointed consumers."

Information Is a Strategic Resource

In the early 1980s, a number-one job title in the United States was the title "clerk"—a sign that the manufacturing-based economy was being eroded by an information-based economy. Today, the second most common job title is "professional," including lawyers, teachers, engineers, reporters, accountants, and librarians. All are information workers.

In today's society, information is our primary strategic resource. Today's PCs, for example, are as powerful as old-fashioned mainframes, and today's mainframes are capable of storing hundreds of times as much information as they have in the past. Knowledge is being generated at an exponentially growing rate. As just one example, more than 6,000 scientific papers are published each day. The problem in today's society is not a lack of information but keeping track of all of it.

Today's marketers are learning the power of information. For instance, they can find out consumers' recent purchases of their products and those of competitors. They can cross-tabulate purchasing history with demographics, psychographics, and financial information to provide accurate lifestyle pictures of any and all customers. Right or wrong, the data is available to any marketer who can afford to purchase it and has the technology to store and manipulate it. Until very recently, the task of organizing and using all of this varied data in a meaningful way proved to be nearly impossible. Today, however, database technology provides a solution. Moreover, the costs of managing data as well as of collecting it have become lower, allowing many marketers to establish their own information- or data-driven marketing programs.

What Today's Database Marketing Can Do

Only the most inexperienced salesperson would pitch all of his or her prospects in the same way, with the same solution. Experienced sales professionals realize that, as individuals, each of us has our own unique set of needs and wants, and therefore is likely to be influenced by sales approaches that are tailored to our unique situation. By its very definition, mass marketing treats all potential customers the same way. This has always been a compromise, because as individuals we have more differences than similarities and, as noted earlier, we are becoming more and more diverse all the time.

In the past, it has been extremely difficult for marketers to address those differences. With the decline of personal selling due to high cost and decreasing effectiveness, the marketer's only other choice has been to address, through the mass market, target segments. The following example illustrates the limitations of marketing to segments. Having defined the typical user of dishwashing detergent as a female householder, age 25 to 40, with a household income of $15,000 to $50,000, suppose marketers rush to develop messages and select media that most appeal to that target segment. Unfortunately, using this aggregate model leads to inherent waste and missed opportunities. Many men, for example, shop for and use dishwashing liquid, and many female householders buy little or none of the product.

With database technology, marketers have, for the first time, the capability to address their customers not as aggregate statistics but as flesh-and-blood individuals. Today's extensive database programs allow marketers to do what the old-fashioned storekeepers of the 1800s did—get to know their customers on a personal, one-to-one basis.

While the shopkeeper may have had only 50, 100, or 200 customers, today's marketers can track their customers as individuals even if they number 50,000,000 . . . and all at an affordable cost.

Through database marketing, you have:

- **The ability to target marketing efforts only to those people likely to be interested.** This targeted approach reduces the waste inherent in any mass-media advertising or blanket direct mail campaign, ultimately resulting in a lower prepurchase marketing cost. In addition, consumers are more likely to pay attention to messages that are specifically directed at them. For instance, baby-care information is likely to catch the eye of parents who have just had their first child. The end result: waste is reduced, and marketing costs go down.

- **The ability to create long-term relationships with customers.** During the 21st century, marketers are likely to realize that keeping customers is less expensive—and more important—than continually trying to get new ones. By looking at customers as individuals, marketers can offer messages about products that will be especially appealing, thereby increasing consumer interest and, consequently, brand loyalty. Companies that keep track of consumer buying patterns can offer special incentives such as price promotions only to customers who have ceased buying, thereby encouraging them to resume purchasing without affecting the margins on sales to more constant customers.

- **The ability to offer varied messages to different consumers.** Recognizing that consumers are individuals, marketers may use database technology to target different consumers with different messages for the same product. For example, Metamucil currently runs one advertising campaign in senior-citizen magazines that promotes the product's laxative effects. Another campaign in health magazines emphasizes the benefits of the product's fiber in a balanced diet. Many major companies such as Coca-Cola and McDonald's, recognizing the differences in how white and black audiences look at advertising, employ specialty agencies to create advertising specifically targeted toward black consumers. The Canada tourism board sends out two separate mailings—one to sporting enthusiasts interested in skiing, backpacking, and other outdoor activities, and another to persons interested in the country's rich culture and history. As database marketing becomes more widely understood and used, such programs are likely to become more common and sophisticated.

- **An advantage in distributing products.** Targeting customers individually is likely to result in a large base of people who are presold on products, and who will look for them at the point of sale, thereby making it easier to obtain distribution. If products are to be sold through direct mail, targeting the right people with the right message is likely to result in fewer pieces being tossed aside and a higher response rate.

- **Increased knowledge about customers.** Marketers who promote to a mass audience usually know very little about their customers. The little demographic and psychographic information they do have is based upon specialized, expensive surveys, focus groups, and other research studies designed to give companies a sense of "who really buys this stuff." With a targeted, well-run database program in place, much information about consumers (such as demographics, psychographics, and past-purchase behavior) can already be in place. Marketers can thereby easily and regularly access in-depth, census-like information about their customers, allowing them to make more informed marketing decisions.

Database Marketing Drives Business Growth

The bottom line for marketers is that there are only three ways to grow a business:

1. Keep your current customers and get them to increase their purchases of your products
2. Take customers away from your competition
3. Generate first-time category buyers

In order to succeed, marketers must develop a strategy to focus on all three areas at the same time. The problem used to be how to identify and reach the individuals in each of the three categories. Today, with the availability of technology and information about customers, data-driven marketing has surfaced as the most efficient and effective way to reach target markets with a message that will accomplish these strategic business objectives. Capturing basic, relevant information about customers and potential customers provides the ability to identify them, communicate with them, and capture sales, while providing measurable results of marketing effectiveness.

Thus, the strategic role of database marketing is to help identify target audiences and facilitate an ongoing relationship (through product sales) between those audiences and the marketer. The database becomes the heart of the marketing intelligence system. It allows the marketer to monitor the relationship between products and customers on an ongoing basis. And it provides a unique ability to communicate with any target audience segment of customers on demand.

Database Marketing Is a Cost-Effective Alternative

One of the most frequently asked questions is whether database marketing will prove itself cost-effective. Suppose your product sells for only $1.29. Is database technology still a worthwhile investment? The answer is that whatever your product or service, you cannot afford to ignore the unique ability of database marketing to capture information on your customers. Given the need to measure return on advertising investment and the general decline of mass media performance (and its corresponding increase in cost), direct communication with customers is now the only truly cost-effective option. The advancing technology in both computer hardware and software programs, the declining cost of computer time, and the complexity and sophistication of information available have made database-driven marketing a viable alternative for any marketer. Add to the equation the ability of database marketing to ease problems with distribution and build long-term relationships with individual customers for the first time, and it is obvious that marketers must invest in database technology if they are to remain competitive.

Once the commitment to database marketing is made, marketers start to view customers in an entirely different perspective. No longer is a customer viewed only from the perspective of the last purchase and promotion, but from the value of the total future sales potential or lifetime value of the customer to the brand. Only at this point is the true potential of database-driven marketing reached. The database becomes a resource that drives ongoing sales efforts. And the only limit to the value of the database is the quality of the customer information it holds.

Information Really Is Power

> I know who my customer is. She is aged 18 to 34, married, has at least two children, and lives in the suburbs. She and her husband own their home and make at least $25,000. However, when I go to retail and watch who takes my products off the shelf . . . they never look the same as the description suggests.

The marketer who said this will remain anonymous. However, he or she could be anyone working with 1980s data and information resources.

Just as Henry Ford and other industrialists did at the turn of the 20th century, marketers today stand at a crossroads. Most companies will, undoubtedly, continue to cast their nets at the mass market, at least for a while, because new systems are not yet perfected and because it is difficult to make integral changes in any organization. Those marketers will continue to face the same problems they are coping with today—only those problems are likely to become intensified over the next few years, as competition becomes tougher and more sophisticated. For marketers with the vision to recognize the future and the spirit to move toward it, however, today's marketing realities present a unique opportunity. For them database marketing will be one of the tools that can be used to more effectively communicate on a one-to-one basis with millions of constantly changing, immensely varied consumers. In an age in which marketing battles are won or lost not on brains or creativity or even experience, but on the power of information, database marketing is the one tool that gives marketers an edge over their competitors. Those who use information wisely will be several steps ahead of the game, and will lead all the others into the future of marketing.

What Database Marketing Is . . . and How It Works

C H A P T E R **3**

The ABCs of Database Marketing

It means rediscovering how to talk to individuals in a way that many in a new generation of marketers have never learned . . . And as in any good relationship it means learning to listen as well as talk—turning the usual advertising monologue into a dialogue, finding new ways to hear what your customers are trying to tell you, and responding to them.

Stan Rapp and Tom Collins,
The Great Marketing Turnaround
(Prentice-Hall, Englewood Cliffs, NJ, 1990)

All consumers are not alike. This is the basis for data-driven marketing. Its premise is that by gathering, maintaining, and analyzing information about your customers and/or prospects, you will be able to implement more effective and efficient marketing communications programs.

A database is a collection of data about your customers and prospects that affects what and how you sell to them. At its simplest, it can be a list such as a phone directory in your sales notebook. At its most complex, linking together all the information necessary to manage a business.

As a resource, a database can become a very important tool for your marketing programs. But, no matter how important it becomes, databases do not do marketing . . . marketers do!

This is why we define the process as data-driven marketing. A database provides the resources for a new generation of marketers to perform marketing surgery. With the tools of their trade—data, technology, and statistical techniques—database marketers communicate to individuals, not to aggregate market segments. Through their databases, they refine their skills, learning to predict the purchase behavior of their targets. In other words, data-driven marketing is practiced by database marketers.

Strategically, the role of database marketing is to help identify a marketer's target audiences and facilitate the ongoing relationship between the target audience and the marketer. Thus, the database becomes the heart of the marketer's intelligence system. It allows the marketer to monitor the ongoing relationship between his or her products and customers and to communicate with any target audience segment on demand.

What Is Database Marketing?

Database marketing is a customer-based, information-intensive, and long-term−oriented marketing method. A database can be used to link and guide current marketing efforts as well as to build an overall body of information to direct future efforts.

Database marketing always includes the following:

- A comprehensive collection of interrelated data . . .
- Serving multiple applications . . .
- Allowing timely and accurate retrieval of information.

It links information related to the customer including purchase transactions, products purchased, promotions, media, geodemographics, lifestyles, demographics, and financial characteristics.

Classically, database marketing has been defined as looking at tactics or at marketing contacts one at a time. Modern database marketing uses the database as a cornerstone of ongoing marketing efforts.

Databases Can Be Passive or Active

Use of the database is either passive or active depending on the nature of the marketing activity. A passive database (Figure 3-1) follows classical marketing thinking. A marketing effort delivers results that are stored in a database, and future marketing efforts draw only from the same data. The marketing pattern is tactic, capture, tactic. The current marketing effort is not influenced by previous efforts.

An active database (Figure 3-2), on the other hand, functions as a strategic resource. The database is the heart of the marketing decision-making process. It provides the single source of information for developing the strategic plan for a data-driven marketing program. Using the database, target marketing programs are developed to meet marketing objectives.

These programs are then executed and their results updated into the database. The strategic loop then starts over again.

Figure 3-1   Passive Database

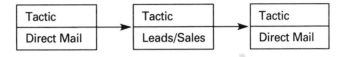

Figure 3-2   Active Database

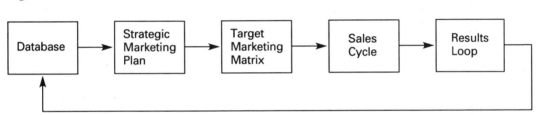

There is more than one way to do database marketing. Many large marketers start their database efforts in a passive, tactically driven role, and later expand to a more active, strategic database effort when it makes sense for the marketing application.

Database Marketing Requires a New Set of Skills

The implementation of a database marketing program requires certain sets of skills. These skills fall into four groups:

- Marketing skills
- Technology skills
- Statistical skills
- Data management skills.

Each set of skills is newly defined in the emerging field of database marketing. For example, marketing has been classically defined by the four Ps: product, price, promotion, and place. Data-driven marketing also requires an understanding of how a body of customer data (the database) can affect the sales process, distribution, and communications efforts.

Marketing Skills

The marketing function encompasses both strategic consulting and creative execution. Strategic consulting must evaluate the business situation of the marketer and determine what role data-driven marketing can fulfill, if any. This means evaluating the short- and long-term communications alternatives, distribution alternatives, product mix, and marketing information requirements. The role of the database is molded to the unique sales communications process for each marketer. In other words, a database marketing strategy maximizes the concept that each customer or prospect is unique. The implementation of that strategy is the development of a series of communications programs based on the unique characteristics of the customers or prospects who receive them.

Technology Skills

The world of database technology changes quickly. Almost any marketing application can now be accomplished using either relational or nonrelational technology. The power of micro- and minicomputers to manage large amounts of information is also rapidly increasing. An organization using database marketing services must be able to understand and manage the technical development and programming process in developing its marketing database. This process requires skills with personal, mini-, and mainframe computers as well as data platforms such as relational and structured environments. (The technology of database marketing is discussed in Chapters 7 and 8.) While a database may be implemented by a third party, the developer must be able to lead the process and determine the best way to meet the marketing requirements. This process becomes more complicated by the need to choose among the many types of computers and software applications.

Statistical Skills

Once the database is developed, statistical skills move the database marketing effort forward. Data does not have value until it can be accessed in a way that creates value. Data segmentation and modeling skills allow the marketer to refine the database-driven communications process. Statistics allow the marketer to accomplish the following:

1. Mail to smaller segments of customers or prospects with increased profitability or no sales decline,

2. Predict consumer behavior based upon past behavior and other characteristics such as demographics and lifestyles,

3. Identify prospects who mimic the characteristics of customers,

4. Identify new opportunities that are either over- or underrepresented in your database or suggest new products or services,

5. Identify and monitor the value of a customer over time.

It is only through statistical manipulation that a database will reach its full potential as a marketing resource.

Data Management Skills

Managing the choice of which data is kept in a marketing database has become a science. Few marketers are blessed with having too much information about their customers or prospects. Most struggle to gain only the basic demographic data. Through a strategic process known as *source data strategy,* a marketer can, over time, collect the most useful amount and types of data about customers or prospects. This strategy requires review of the organization's ability to gather data via internal, external, and custom methods. Then via testing, statistical analysis, and communications programs the information in the database is balanced to meet the organization's marketing information requirements.

To develop a database marketing program, you as the marketer must acquire these basic skills. Investment in technology is not enough. It is the correct balance of data, technology, and statistical analysis skills that allow a database to become a marketing resource.

Database Marketing Is a Communications Process

The process of database-driven communications or target marketing can be simplified into a model that, with variations, can represent any data-driven marketing situation (Figure 3-3). The model has three phases:

- Identification of customers or prospects,
- Communication, and
- Capture of resulting information.

The identification phase involves accessing the database to target the appropriate customers or prospects for the desired program. Data sources for target identification include customer data, overlaid enhancement data, and customer-developed data such as survey data. (Source data strategy is discussed in Chapter 6.) The next step is to develop the appropriate marketing communications effort based upon the requirements of the business and the targeting program. This process is both strategic and creative. The results of the marketing effort are then captured and updated into the database to increase the body of information, revise targeting and identification programs, and provide marketing information. The process is just that simple and just that complex:

Figure 3-3   Database Communications Model

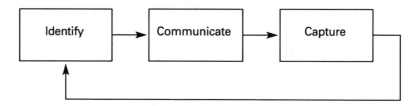

Each step of the communications process requires different skills. In the identification phase, the marketer must be able to select data that has the characteristics necessary to identify appropriate customers or prospects for a program. Statistical techniques must be used to examine the accumulated data and select target customers/prospects. Data processing technology must be used to access the customer/prospect for the communications effort.

The communications phase requires strategic consulting to develop the correct type of marketing effort based upon the relationship of the customer/prospect and the marketer. Creative skill is required to develop an effective communications vehicle (such as direct mail, broadcast, or print) to reach the customer/prospect effectively.

In the capture phase, technology is required to manage information that results from the marketing communications effort, and data skills are needed to maximize the value of the customer characteristics recorded.

Where to Start in Database Marketing

With a definition of database marketing and database communications and an understanding of the basic skill sets necessary to be successful in database marketing, we can now move on to how to determine where to start. There are no "secrets" to database marketing, only the combination of several important building blocks to create a valuable resource.

The real value of this book is that we have developed a methodology outlining the three major types of database marketing and the requirements to develop a program in each. In each section of the book, the building blocks of data, technology, and statistical analysis will be discussed in terms of the specific application. Thus, when you finish with the book, you should have a good indication of the correct application of database marketing for your business situation and an understanding of the considerations that you face and the combination of building blocks required to be successful with your database application.

Three Points of Entry into Database Marketing

An organization's technical database solution should be designed around its marketing requirements. When and how information is to be used is the most important point in dictating the structure of a marketing database. Because most marketing applications are unique, it is possible that there are as many different technical solutions available as there are marketing programs. However, most database marketing applications fall into three basic types or points of entry into database marketing (Figure 3-4). The three entry points are: historical data management, marketing intelligence, and the integrated business resource. As we explore each point of entry, think of your business situation and which point of entry comes closest to meeting your requirements.

Figure 3-4   Points of Entry into Database Marketing

Point of Entry #1: Historical Data Management Systems

Historical data management databases are used primarily to track data captured from tactical marketing programs (this is passive database usage).

Generally speaking, the data captured is limited to name, address, lead/ sales activity, and promotion effort information. Output from this type of database includes reports for tracking of program effectiveness and selections for mailing. An example of a historical database would be a marketer, such as a retailer or dealer, that uses direct mail promotions to generate leads. The marketer is interested in capturing information on the interest of the prospect and evaluating the effectiveness of the promotion that generated the leads. The marketer then may or may not follow the lead through the sales cycle via a sales force, retailer, or dealer. If sales results are received, they are updated into the database. The database then serves as a source to extract names for future mailings or other marketing communications tactics. Basically the system flow is:

Figure 3-5

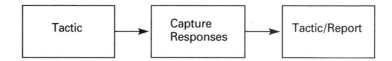

Thus, a historical database is used to manage historical data received about customers or prospects.

Point of Entry #2: Marketing Intelligence Databases

The second entry point, marketing intelligence, builds on the information captured in a historical data management system. The major distinction between this category and the first is that the database allows the marketer to analyze the data for detailed marketing decisions. A marketing intelligence system captures a greater array of data than basic customer information. Via a source data strategy (discussed in Chapter 6), additional information on customers or prospects may be added into the database to enhance the ability of the marketer to understand customers and their purchase behavior. The goal of a marketing intelligence system is to learn from current and past customer/prospect behavior as tracked into the database and then predict the propensity for future consumer purchase behavior. An example would be a bank that captures historical data about its customers, their accounts, and current transactions. With the overlay of related data available from outside sources, the bank may be able to develop programs to predict the likelihood that a customer with one type of account will be interested in another type of account. The flow of an active database is as follows (Figure 3-6):

Figure 3-6

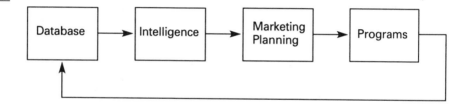

The database drives an intelligence or learning process that provides information for marketing decision making and thus "smart" or targeted communications programs.

Entry Point #3: The Integrated Business Resource

An integrated business resource serves as the entire information resource for an organization. This is accomplished by integrating all key business information sources or functions in the organization. Examples of the functions include finance, customer service, distribution, inventory, manufacturing, research, and marketing. Generally, businesses using integrated resources are driven by the database. Examples of these business categories include insurance companies, mutual funds, banks, and catalog companies. A system flow for an integrated database is as follows:

Figure 3-7

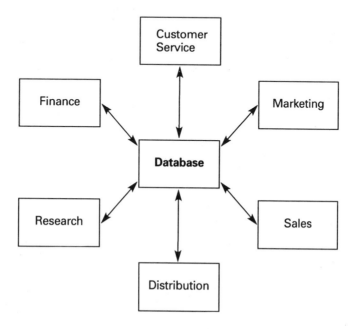

In the integrated business resource, information is gathered from all relevant departments and shared with all departments. The collective data provides greater intelligence and decision-making capabilities than would any piece of the whole.

Assessing Your Point of Entry

At this stage, you may understand exactly which point of entry matches your application or you may feel that your situation doesn't fit any of the three. If your application does not fit exactly into one of the three points of entry, don't worry. In reality, the three points of entry are nothing more than three points along a continuum of marketing applications and technology. From one of the three entry points, the marketer can customize the appropriate technology to develop a database that is unique to the organization's requirements. In Chapters 7 and 8, we will discuss the specific technical characteristics associated with each point of entry into database marketing. The purpose of these points of entry is to serve as benchmarks to match an organization's marketing requirements with options for database structure. In short, the custom solution starts with a technology that is appropriate to the need or application.

Determining Your Database Requirements

Once you have compared your potential database application to the three points of entry to database marketing, it is time to look at the considerations that will govern your decision to proceed with development of a database. You must evaluate the cost, effect, and requirements of a decision to proceed with database marketing at or near one of the three points of entry. Five major categories of requirements will affect your decision to move forward. To help visualize the process, we have developed a decision matrix which facilitates comparison of the five database requirements categories and the three basic points of entry.

The five database requirement categories, illustrated in Figure 3-8, are:

- Marketing requirements,
- Organizational requirements,
- Information management requirements,
- Technology requirements, and
- Financial requirements.

Figure 3-8   Database Marketing Decision-Making Matrix

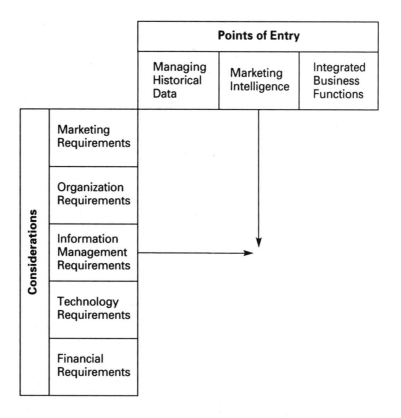

Table 3-1 compares these requirements and the three points of entry into database marketing.

Marketing Requirements

Basic to the marketing decision is the intended use of the database. Will it be an active or passive database structure? Earlier we discussed that an active database drives the strategic process. This requires more information and technology to provide the information back to you in a way that facilitates your marketing program. Chapter 4 details fifteen ways to use a database marketing program and compares each application to the corresponding point of entry. The decision criteria for relating marketing requirements to a point of entry are outlined in Table 3-1.

Table 3-1   Database Marketing Point of Entry

Point of Entry		
Historical Data Management	**Marketing Intelligence**	**Integrated Business Resources**
Marketing Requirements		
1. Capture and record historical customer data	Develop profiles of today's best customers Use customer information to market more effectively to current customer base Find more people like today's best customers (using internal and external data)	Identify tomorrow's customers as well as future market segments and opportunities
2. Record who responds to promotions	Understand why people respond	Create customers and future response
3. Deliver communications/ promotion with little or no customer knowledge	Deliver communications/ promotion with some customer knowledge	Deliver communications/ promotion with total customer knowledge

Point of Entry		
Historical Data Management	**Marketing Intelligence**	**Integrated Business Resources**
4. Document today's customer-service problems	Solve today's customer-service problems	Deal with tomorrow's customer-service problems
5. Monitor performance	Respond to a changing environment	Initiate change
6. Database operations produce little or no corporate growth	Database operations produce some corporate growth	Database operations responsible for high corporate growth
7. Focus on response rate	Focus on repeat business	Focus on lifetime value

Organizational Requirements

8. Low need to provide integration	Moderate need to provide integration	High need to provide integration
9. Low operational linkage	Moderate operational linkage	High operational linkage
10. Specific plans	Multiple plans	General plans

(Table 3-1 cont.)

Point of Entry		
Historical Data Management	**Marketing Intelligence**	**Integrated Business Resources**
11. Short-range planning	Medium-range planning	Long-range planning
12. Action planning	Business planning	Corporate planning
13. Decentralized	Polycentralized	Centralized
14. Functional managers in each division can initiate database operations	Division managers can initiate database operations	Board of directors and chief executive officer can initiate database operations
15. Generally well understood upon introduction of database project	Somewhat understood upon introduction of database project	Not well understood upon introduction of database project
16. Short learning curve	Medium learning curve	Long learning curve

Point of Entry		
Historical Data Management	Marketing Intelligence	Integrated Business Resources

Information Management Requirements

17. High level of data processing is based on assumed low uncertainty of task and environment	Moderate level of data processing is based on assumed low uncertainty of task and environment	Low level of data processing is based on assumed low uncertainty of task and environment
18. Low level of information sharing and coordination	Moderate level of information sharing and coordination	High level of information sharing and coordination
19. Low level of problem-solving is based on assumed high uncertainty of task and environment	Moderate level of problem-solving is based on assumed high uncertainty of task and environment	High level of problem-solving based on assumed high uncertainty of task and environment
20. Routine programming	Somewhat routine programming	Nonroutine programming
21. Low data diversity	Moderate data diversity	High data diversity
22. Simple data format	Somewhat complex data format	Complex data format

(Table 3-1 cont.)

Point of Entry		
Historical Data Management	**Marketing Intelligence**	**Integrated Business Resources**
23. Stable variables	Somewhat stable variables	Unstable variables
24. Low variation in management specifications	Moderate variation in management specifications	High variation in management specifications
25. Low differentiation	Moderate differentiation	High differentiation
26. Very similar to competitors' databases	Somewhat similar to competitors' databases	Not similar to competitors' databases

Technology Requirements

27. Generic, static system design	Partially customized, somewhat interactive system design	Customized, highly interactive, dynamic system design
28. No awareness that design process has occurred	Some awareness that design process occurs	Awareness that design process occurs
29. Hardware represents initial investment	Software represents major investment	Marketing talent represents major investment

Point of Entry

Historical Data Management	Marketing Intelligence	Integrated Business Resources
30. Technical orientation	Analytical orientation	Marketing orientation
31. Data definition becomes primary concern	Data manipulation becomes primary concern	Data integrity becomes primary concern

Financial Requirements

32. High initial investment and low ongoing costs	Low initial investment and moderate ongoing costs	Moderate initial investment and high ongoing costs
33. Low return on investment	Moderate return on investment	High return on investment
34. Single source funding	Multiple source funding	Corporation-wide funding
35. Low likelihood of generating new business and revenue	Moderate likelihood of generating new business and revenue	High likelihood of generating new business and revenue
36. Prevents competitive disadvantage	May provide moderate competitive advantage	Establishes sustainable competitive advantage

Organizational Requirements

The organizational considerations center on Who? What? and How much? Who will be using the database? How many individuals, what is their skill level, and how many departments do they represent? What different information requirements are represented by the various users of the database? How often will the users access the system? Will various groups or departments use only parts of the database, and do you want to control access to the data? Table 3-1 outlines some of the organizational considerations for each point of entry.

Information Management Requirements

The information management requirements focus on the data or information that is kept in the database. Chapter 6 focuses on the source data strategy that allows a marketer to develop the correct amount of information in the database. Some of the data considerations that affect the choice of point of entry are shown in Table 3-1.

Technology Requirements

The technology requirements are the technological considerations required to develop, manage, and access information to optimize the marketing decision making process. Chapters 7 and 8 focus on the technical decisions required and the technology options available for database marketing. Table 3-1 shows some of the technological considerations and how they relate to each point of entry.

Financial Requirements

Finally, a cost is associated with each activity related to database marketing. Different requirements for marketing, organizational access, information, and technology impact the cost of the database program. As each system is different based upon the unique marketing requirements of a marketer, the costs will be unique also. Table 3-1 lists financial considerations related to the three points of entry.

Now you have an understanding of the considerations necessary to determine where your marketing application fits along the continuum of the three points of entry. The following chapters will give you greater insight into various aspects of these requirements. You will then be ready to review the requirements in terms of your organization's marketing needs and to focus on the appropriate point of entry for your database marketing efforts.

C H A P T E R 4

15 Ways to Use a Marketing Database

Question: What type of marketing program works best by using a marketing database?

Answer: Almost any program, with two conditions: One—The marketer wants to target communications directly to the audience segment that he or she desires to sell; Two—The marketer sees value in creating an ongoing dialog with the consumer based upon capturing and recording relevant information about that consumer.

Targeting + Dialog = Database-Driven Marketing Programs

Database-driven marketing programs are geared to making and keeping customers. If you target your product to the correct consumer with the correct offer, you will make a sale. If you reinforce that sale and keep them happy, your customers will keep buying over time. Database-driven marketing programs are customer driven, not sales driven. Make no mistake, however—like the corner grocer who knew his customers' names, if you are customer driven, sales will follow.

15 Ways to Use Your Database

In this chapter, we will explore 15 ways to implement database-driven marketing communications programs. We choose the words *database-driven* because a database is the resource that allows you to implement highly targeted and dialog-driven marketing programs—programs that will allow you to practice customer-driven marketing.

Each application we explore will be discussed in terms of the database continuum and the points of entry at which each program can be practically implemented. All of the following applications are being practiced today by marketers using databases to drive their communications programs. The fifteen database-driven marketing applications we will review describe how you will:

1. Identify your best customers,
2. Develop new customers,
3. Deliver a message consistent with product usage,
4. Reinforce consumer purchase decisions,
5. Cross-sell and complementary-sell products,
6. Apply three-tiered communications,
7. Improve delivery of sales promotion,
8. Refine the marketing process,
9. Increase the effectiveness of distribution channel marketing,
10. Maintain equity,
11. Establish a management resource,
12. Take advantage of stealth communications,
13. Conduct customer, product, and marketing research,
14. Personalize customer service, and
15. Provide program synergy and integration.

1. Identify Your Best Customers

The most important value of a marketing database is to track customers and their relationship to your business. Most often, this relates to the products and services that they have purchased or inquired about. In order to identify your best customers, you need to be able to look at customer data using either recency, frequency, and monetary analysis (RFM) or comparison analysis.

RFM Analysis

RFM, or recency, frequency, and monetary analysis, assumes that your database is capable of tracking customer transaction data. How many times has a customer purchased your product? How much money has the customer spent per purchase and over time? How recently has the customer made a purchase? This data will allow you to build a simple equation to identify "best customers" based upon the frequency and sales dollars that they have spent with your business (see Chapter 10). RFM data can also be used to create a lifetime value model on customers. Lifetime value not only looks at how important a customer is currently to your business, but projects the value of that customer over a period of years. With this information, a marketer can not only determine which customers have the best potential, but also how much he or she can market to these customers over time and still maximize profits.

Comparison Analysis

If customer purchase transaction data is not available, then other data can be used to compare customers. If you can identify a segment of customers in your database as "good customers" by any means (such as by survey, purchase data, response, or word of mouth), then you can find a way to compare the identified customer segment with the rest of your customers. This can be accomplished by overlaying externally available demographic data on customer data and finding additional customers already in your database that look like your identified "good" customers.

There are three major benefits to identifying your best customers with a database. First, if your goal is to increase sales, you will save money by communicating only with your best customers. By eliminating unproductive customer segments, you can control costs and maintain response. Second, you can increase response and thus efficiency of marketing efforts by identifying more new customers. Third, you can create customer loyalty by acknowledging the relationship that your best customers have with your company. This can be accomplished through ongoing communications programs that cost minimal dollars and reap great rewards in loyalty.

As we mentioned above, identifying your best customers is a key function at all points in the database continuum. In historical data management, customers' past purchase behavior is analyzed and best customers identified based upon past promotion and sales efforts tracked by the database. In marketing intelligence and business resource databases, transactional data and overlay of enhancement data allow for current behavior analysis as well as past purchase behavior analysis of best customers.

2. Develop New Customers

For most marketers, a database is a resource to track current customer activity. As such, it is a built-in research lab. By conducting research on your captive database of customers, you can gain valuable insight into characteristics about them that relate to the purchase of your products and services. This insight translates into a customer profile. We will explore two types of new customer development efforts: finding new customers that look like current customers and identifying competitors' customers.

Finding New Customers That Look Like Current Customers

Generally speaking, if marketers want to target new customers they look to available commercial mailing lists. For business-to-business marketers, these lists include Dun & Bradstreet and American Business Information (ABI). For consumer marketers they include lists from Donnelley, Metromail, or R. L. Polk. These lists are selectable by demographic criteria. Business-to-business demographics include size, sales volume, number of employees, and so on. Consumer demographics include age, income, family size, motor vehicles owned, education, and so on.

Most marketing databases contain a wealth of data on the customer's relationship with the marketer. Information such as recency, frequency, and monetary data on customer purchases is recorded. While this data is very important to determining how valuable a customer is relative to other customers, it rarely helps to select outside prospects from commercially available lists.

Consumer demographics are available for use to enhance or overlay on existing customer data (see Chapter 6 on data strategy). With conventional research and analysis techniques, externally available enhancement data can provide a detailed demographic customer profile that is a powerful tool in effectively targeting outside lists. In most cases, with testing and refinement, the costs of testing, research, and data overlay are more than covered by the increased targeting ability and resulting sales.

Identifying Competitors' Customers

For many marketers, especially those with mature products or in established product categories, the mission is to identify and capture a competitor's customers or identify customers that are new to a category. A technique that has become increasingly popular is surveys or questionnaires.

Marketers will develop surveys or questionnaires for proprietary use or join in cooperative efforts that are mailed or bundled in FSIs in very large quantities. The goal of the surveys is to identify brand, category, and frequency usage. For example, a major consumer products marketer could identify all purchasers of children's cereal, the brands used, and the frequency of usage by household. If a household is identified as a user of a competitive brand, a switch strategy is implemented via direct mail. If a loyal user is identified, a retention strategy is implemented. All of this activity is accomplished under the secrecy of the marketer's database. While this technique is expensive due to its two-step nature (first the identification of customers and then the marketing communications strategy), it becomes a powerful way of building both a customer list and a list of your competitors' customers.

3. Deliver a Message Consistent with Product Usage

This technique is probably the most obvious, but most seldom used. Even at its most basic level, a database will allow you to track your customers' relationship to your products and services.

Your database allows you to segment your targeted marketing communications based upon each customer's purchases. The most traditional approach is to develop a segmented communications strategy. The following is an example of a strategy developed for three customer segments based upon their purchase behavior.

- **New or infrequent customers.** Develop targeted communications programs that stimulate a repeat purchase until your research shows that the customer has migrated to a regular pattern of purchases. The database can track each purchase.

- **Moderate usage customers.** Develop a communications program that offers less direct incentive and more reinforcement.

- **Heavy usage customers.** Design targeted communications around loyalty and reinforcement programs rather than price promotion.

4. Reinforce Consumer Purchase Decisions

Almost everyone likes to be noticed and recognized. The most powerful words in sales should be "Thank you!" The second should be "You made the right decision." A database offers the opportunity to reach out to your customers with two powerful reinforcement programs based on these words:

- **Thank you.** It does not matter what you sell—mutual funds, cars, electronics, cereal, or flowers—say "thank you" to your customers based upon what they purchased and remind them how important they are to your business.

- **You made the right decision.** If the consumer purchase decision was major, reinforce it with some positive information about the product and why the decision to deal with you was the best one. For example: Mr. Jackson, Thank you for buying a SAAB. Did you know that your SAAB has the highest consumer rating . . . and the lowest problems . . . Also if you have any problems, call me personally and, by the way, you get a free loaner for service. . . .

5. Cross-Sell and Complementary-Sell Products

The heart of this application is again research. By developing profiles of customers' key characteristics and matching those to profiles of product users, you can better match product and customer. This process will accomplish two major marketing objectives by providing opportunities to cross-sell and complementary-sell.

Cross-Sell Opportunity

Products and brands, like people, have profiles. In fact, a brand may have several different profiles based upon level of usage, size, or distinct differences in the way the product is used by the target group. A database will allow you to match product profiles and customer profiles to cross-sell customers other products that match their demographic, lifestyle, or behavioral characteristics. For example, a customer who fits the profile for active-lifestyle-conscious products by either purchasing one or matching the target audience profile is a likely candidate for marketing communications of an entire family of products in the same category. Another example from banking is that a mortgage holder may match the profile for a money market account as well as the profile for a home equity loan.

Complementary-Sell Opportunity

Products or groups of products not originally considered marketable for the same target audience can be regrouped, repackaged, or remarketed based on the identification of similar customer profiles. Target audience profiles may lead to development of new products or extension of existing product lines.

6. Apply Three-Tiered Communications

By understanding the relative value of each customer in the database, a marketer can evaluate communications alternatives in terms of return on communications investment. Traditionally, this involves classifying customers and prospects into three or more tiers. The tiers represent the level of buying power the customer represents to your product or service. Once identified by tier, a customer can be targeted by the appropriate message and amount of communications. The process of classification is accomplished by comparing customers and prospects to a profile of customers with high, medium, or low sales potential.

A business-to-business example offers the best case for tiered communications. A business-to-business marketer's precious resource is the sales force. Today's business environment is characterized by increased competition, longer sales cycles, and dramatically rising cost to maintain a sales force in the field. Thus, business marketers want to maximize the performance of their field sales forces. By analyzing the profiles of high-, medium-, and low-potential customers, each new business prospect can be evaluated in terms of the most effective use of resources based upon potential for a sale. This process leads to development of a three-tiered structure for communicating with potential prospects.

If a prospect is evaluated as having high sales potential and thus falls into tier one, targeted communications are used to introduce and support the salesperson's contact and the sales cycle with the prospect. In this tier, the salesperson drives the sales process. If a prospect is evaluated as tier two, targeted communications are used to evaluate the customer's level of interest before a salesperson is introduced. Thus the salesperson is focused on the right individual and product when he or she first walks into the prospect's door. In tier three, the sales potential is judged to be lower than the requirements necessary to assign a salesperson to the prospect. The sales process is handled via targeted communications options such as direct mail, telemarketing, or an inside sales force.

Almost all products and services, both business-to-business and consumer, can benefit from a tiered selling strategy. Exceptions include products that are so commodised that developing distinct profiles based upon level of usage is not possible.

7. Improve Delivery of Sales Promotion

As previously mentioned, environmental changes in marketing have opened the door for alternative methods of delivery of sales promotion. Traditionally, most sales promotion delivery has been via mass media or point of sale. For consumer products marketers, FSIs (free standing inserts in newspapers) have been a primary delivery vehicle. However, with increasing costs, lower circulation, changing lifestyles, lower response rates and higher misredemption rates, FSIs are returning a lower return per dollar for marketers. Databases offer consumer products marketers with a cost-effective alternative to target only promotion-responsive customers with known interest in a brand or category. With lower computer costs for information storage and new personalization techniques to track coupon effectiveness, targeted coupon mailings driven by a promotionally developed database are becoming an important marketing tool for many marketers.

8. Refine the Marketing Process

While a database exists if customers' names and addresses are captured, database marketing occurs only when dialog is created with these customers. In most cases that dialog includes feedback resulting from marketing efforts. The success of data-driven marketing requires tracking and evaluation of each activity that the database generates. It is only through this process that intelligence and an understanding of the purchasing behavior of your customers can be achieved.

Statistical techniques are key to this process. Sound research will develop test programs that can be evaluated and are economically viable. The use of statistical analysis techniques to develop customer profiles and to model and evaluate a database for marketing planning is the key to successful database marketing.

Via testing, statistical research, and targeted communications, a database can become a strategic resource that can help you evaluate all aspects of your marketing efforts. By allowing you to understand at the household or individual level your target audiences, the effectiveness of your communications programs, and the ability of your product mix to satisfy your customers' needs, the database will become your most important resource.

9. Increase the Effectiveness of Distribution Channel Marketing

As Figure 4-1 illustrates, several channels of distribution exist for products and services.

Figure 4-1   Multiple Distribution Channels

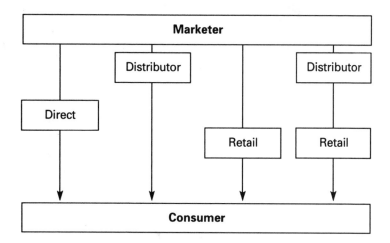

In several, intervening layers such as wholesalers, distributors, or retailers compete with the manufacturer for the consumers' loyalty. Increasingly, we note two important trends: First, many consumer marketers lose touch with the retailers of their products because of the power of an intervening distributor. Second, power retailers (for example, grocers and major department stores) are attempting to establish strong relationships with customers that sometimes occur at the expense of the manufacturer of the product or service.

Database marketing provides an opportunity to equalize both trends. For manufacturers that do not have access directly to customers or retailers, database marketing offers an opportunity to gain insight into who is selling and buying products. This can be accomplished with a source data strategy as proposed in Chapter 6. For marketers who are being preempted by retailers' relationships with the consumer, database marketing provides an opportunity to talk directly to the consumer or to work in constructive alliance with retailers by developing joint communications programs to the manufacturer's known customer base.

Database marketing also offers the opportunity to create a new channel for distribution of products or services. For example, a multistore retailer may develop a catalog to increase sales in areas not covered by the stores. A retail chain selling high-end electronics might develop a mail-order video and audio tape program for customers who purchase VCRs or stereos. A specialty coffee retailer can easily create a mail-order business. The opportunities are limited only by a marketer's creativity.

10. Maintain Brand Equity

For marketers of consumer products, many retailers, and an increasing number of traditional direct marketers, a great deal of time and money is spent in developing and maintaining brand equity. Brand equity is the image or feeling you have as a consumer when you hear about, see, or remember a product. Images come to mind with the words Coke, Kellogg's Frosted Flakes, Crest, Downy fabric softener, Land's End, Neiman Marcus, and Pillsbury, just to name a few. These marketers will go to almost any extremes to ensure that anyone who is involved with their product, from the retailer to promotion to advertising to packaging, is saying the same thing in the same way. It is brand equity that creates the differences in sales between Coke and Pepsi, GM and Ford, McDonald's and Burger King.

Maintaining brand equity control is an increasing problem in multiple-distribution environments. For example, the marketers of Crest or Tide want the consumer to get a certain image of their product, certainly not on the same page with a competitive product. Retailers, on the other hand, are loyal to consumers' desires rather than to a specific product. They may advertise two competing brands in the same ad, hoping to attract users of both products into their stores. To them, a sale is a sale, no matter the brand.

Database marketing allows a marketer to assume complete control over the message that it communicates to its customers. The marketer controls what it says, how it says it, and to whom. This provides an important boost to a product's equity in a competitive multiple-distribution environment.

11. Establish a Management Resource

The question you must ask is, What value does data have to my business? The answer depends on the level of functional integration of marketing related activities in your organization. Data-driven marketing can support more than the traditional marketing requirements. For example:

- Advertising,
- Research,
- Product development,
- Distribution,
- Customer service,
- Media, and more.

By understanding the data and business requirements of each related function area of your organization, you can maximize the three key building blocks to create a resource that will integrate all relevant business functions into your marketing database.

12. Take Advantage of Stealth Communications

A good description of this application comes from a meeting in which a senior executive of a major consumer products company was overheard to say, "A database offers me a way to communicate with my customers without my competition knowing. When I do FSIs, print ads, or television commercials, my competitors know usually before the customer does what I am saying and how. Then they develop a strategy to counter me. However, with database marketing, no one knows but us and the customer. . . . It really is a stealth communications vehicle."

13. Conduct Customer, Product, and Marketing Research

Your database, when used as an intelligence resource, offers a workbench for research. Research on customers, product development, test marketing, media, distribution, evaluation of communications programs, and many other applications unique to your business can be carried out.

Customer Research

Statistical techniques such as those used for customer profile development and segmentation give unique insight into customer purchase behavior. Before databases, consumer marketers could look at customers only as aggregate statistics rather than uniquely as individuals or households. The database offers the opportunity to identify characteristics that lead to purchase behavior and to model both the propensity to purchase and the value of purchase behavior over time.

Product Development Research

By understanding customer profile segments, target audiences, and how both match up to product purchases, a marketer can effectively analyze all aspects of product purchase behavior. For example, product families can be regrouped to take advantage of similar customer profiles. Communications efforts can be redesigned based upon target audience profiles.

New products can be developed for target audiences that are underrepresented in the database. A database can also serve as a platform for analysis of product life cycles.

Test Marketing

Direct marketers have used their databases in test marketing new products and modifications of existing products (including price, packaging, and offer) to target segments for many years. Today, consumer product marketers are simulating traditional test marketing applications on their marketing databases without conducting actual market tests. The result of these efforts will eventually be significant reliance on database-driven test efforts in combination with or instead of actual test marketing. This will decrease costs and create a more private environment for testing and evaluation.

Media Research

Large databases offer fertile environments to provide detailed demographics that will lead to more targeted mass media purchases. Many marketers now look to the concept of brand contacts. Under this strategy, a database of targeted customers can function as a control to decide among the communications options at a brand's disposal, such as awareness media, promotion, or relationship communications. By identifying the target audiences' propensity to purchase (see Application 6) brands can maximize exposure and minimize media expenditure. Several research projects are underway today to correlate mass media buying, syndicated media research data, and the targeting of mass media expenditures.

Distribution Research

Databases allow a marketer to identify customers' addresses and point-of-sale information. Thus marketers can evaluate the effectiveness of entire distribution channels as well as specific points of distribution within a channel. For some marketers, a database provides the only feedback about the retailer or point-of-sale contact with the customer.

For example, a manufacturer can evaluate product movement by channel from a number of perspectives. It can look at the overall channel, evaluate by market, or evaluate by chain or by store. The database can then be used to stimulate sales at any level of distribution by push or pull strategies. Push strategies drive customers to a retailer through product offers, while pull strategies work with the retailer to pull business to stores.

Database marketing also provides the opportunity to test and implement alternative distribution channels. For example: a clothes manufacturer might develop a catalog in addition to retail; a cataloger might develop a retail channel; a retailer might develop a mail-order channel to capture peripheral business from purchasers of specialty products such as high-end electronics or appliances.

Communications Program Evaluation Research

By tracking the result of your communications effort to customers via code, coupon, telephone response, scanner, or other technique, marketers can evaluate the effectiveness of their communications programs. This evaluation will help determine how sophisticated targeting programs can be developed that increase a marketer's return on investment. By evaluating the effectiveness of targeted communications, delivery of promotion, and relationship communications over time, a marketer may place a measurable and budgetable value on current and lifetime communications with customers and prospects.

As you can see, database marketing provides a captive resource for creative evaluation of current and new techniques. The ability to use the database as a research laboratory is limited only by commitment, resources, and the data you capture.

14. Personalize Customer Service

To repeat a theme that business pundits have used over and over, American business has lost touch with customers. The two "magic words," *please* and *thank-you,* can be used in every business situation with powerful results. When a retailer, car dealer, or manufacturer follows up and says "thank-you" or "was your experience a good one," the customer may first be shocked speechless. His or her next thought may be "I'm going back there," just because care was shown.

Just think about it . . . you as a database marketer have a captive resource to provide goodwill and powerful feedback on the purchase process. You know what your customer purchased and where. Follow the following five points of data-driven customer service and you may never lose a customer again.

1. Say "thank-you" to customers for purchasing your product or service. This one act is a powerful relationship builder.

2. Get feedback on the purchase process and customer satisfaction.

3. If the feedback is good, reinforce the purchase decision—let the customer know that he or she has made a smart decision and why.

4. If the feedback is negative, create a system that forces recognition of complaints and give customers feedback that their input was important. (For example, send the customer a copy of your letter to the branch manager.)

5. Communicate every once in a while with the customer without expecting a sale or response. Send helpful tips or a calendar—almost anything will do.

Only you can evaluate how far you can afford to go to implement a data-driven customer service strategy. However, we feel that money spent to personalize customer service will be the best marketing dollars you can spend.

15. Provide Program Synergy and Integration

A database provides synergy and integration for marketers in two ways: by tracking marketing efforts by customer and by guiding the marketing planning process.

The Synergy of Customer-Based Marketing

By tracking all marketing efforts by customer, a marketer can eliminate duplicate, supplemental, and misdirected communications. This creates advertising efficiency in both message consistency and dollar expenditures. This concept works customer by customer. For example, a marketer with a database covering multiple brands can identify and protect loyal users of brand A from other promotions inside the company that might erode this loyalty. Additionally, with a central database, a marketing organization with multiple marketing arms can avoid duplication of efforts against the same customers.

Program Integration

A database provides a strategic platform to maximize the effectiveness of all marketing efforts as parts of the overall marketing plan. If viewed as a strategic resource and the repository of all marketing intelligence, a database can drive the planning process that determines what programs to market to each target audience and with how much overlap. For example, by analysis of a customer database a marketer can plan future activity based on tiered communications and opportunity to cross-sell. Statistically, the marketer can identify propensity to purchase and place a current and future value on each customer. With this completed for each program and customer, a marketer can maximize communications and sales projections via the information contained in the database.

The above 15 database applications represent major uses of database marketing. There are many more. We hope that these examples will stimulate many other creative ideas that are relevant to your business.

C H A P T E R **5**

Database Marketing
in Action

Your business attitude determines your potential for innovation, creativity, even genius, and success in your field.

Thinkertoys, Michael Michalko
(Ten Speed Press, Berkeley, CA 1991)

Now that we have discussed what database marketing is and how it can be applied, let's look at how it is being *used* to improve business productivity. In the nine cases that follow, the names and details of each organization have been changed—to give these marketers the benefit of secrecy (. . . and in some instances to protect the guilty!). As you will remember, stealth is one of the benefits of database marketing. While marketers may be willing to share the fact that they are involved with database marketing, many prefer—for competitive reasons—to keep the details of their programs to themselves.

The Continuum of Database Marketing

The nine cases here have been chosen from among dozens because of their relation to the three basic points of entry into database marketing. After each case is presented, the application is evaluated by its place on the continuum of the three points of entry (Figure 5-1). This is intended to help you find out exactly where *your* company lies on the continuum.

Figure 5-1 The Three Points of Entry along a Continuum of Database Marketing

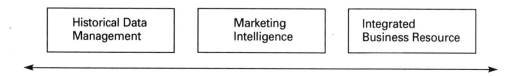

The three points of entry do not necessarily reflect on the quality of the database effort by any of the cases or in your application, but the degree of sophistication of the use of the three key building blocks we will explore in Part III of this book—data, technology, and statistical techniques.

The nine case histories are as follows:

A. Consumer Products, Inc. A major consumer package goods company

B. Big Picture Company. A first-run motion picture developer

C. *Read Me* Magazine. A news magazine

D. Beans & Brew. Local retailer of whole beans and coffee drinks

E. Smart Politician. A local politician

F. Hardware & Things. A "do-it-yourself" hardware retailer

G. WDBM Radio. A contemporary music radio station

H. Slots & More. A Nevada hotel and casino

I. Mail Order Computers. Mail order marketer of computers

We have classified the nine cases (A to I) along the database continuum of the three points of entry as follows:

Figure 5-2

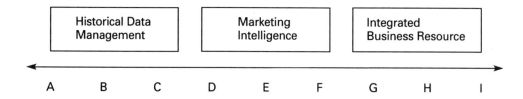

By reviewing the cases, you will get a feel of some applications of database marketing. You will also start to gain an appreciation of the points of entry and the three key building blocks, finding out how they relate to your entry into database marketing.

A. Consumer Products, Inc.

Business Profile

Leading manufacturer and marketer of consumer products ranging from soap to food. Markets over 100 brands representing more than 30 categories of products. Manufactures and distributes via food and other retailers throughout the United States and the world.

Marketing Overview

Traditionally, products are marketed with a three part strategy, including:

- Sales promotion, encouraging trial, switching and increased purchase frequency
- Image advertising, creating and maintaining brand identity and image
- In-store promotions, retail marketing designed to maximize brand exposure to the shopper

Companies such as Consumer Products, Inc. have found the entry into database marketing confusing, to say the least. Products sell at a relatively low price point (under $2.00, for example, for dishwashing liquid) and have a low profit margin. This is compared to the higher-priced and higher-margin products traditionally marketed via a database or through direct marketing. In addition, consumer manufacturers view success not on a item-by-item basis, but in terms of moving multiple cases of product through retailers to millions and millions of consumers. In this manner, a product with a low price point and low profit margin becomes successful. It's simple economy of scale. Economy of scale encourages marketing that reaches the millions rather than the few. Communications are measured in terms of their reach and frequency into the mass market, rather than in terms of the individuals they reach. Database marketing, on the other hand, targets individuals and has a very high cost per thousand compared to TV advertising and other mass media vehicles. It's easy to see why it is so hard for consumer products marketers to make a commitment to database marketing that focuses on a few consumers when they are measured by their ability to move lots of product to masses of consumers.

However, consumer products marketers are facing changing marketing dynamics—changes in consumer purchase behavior, consumer demographics, media costs, and the power of the retailer, to name just a few. To remain competitive, mass marketers must focus on keeping customers and encouraging loyalty. Even more importantly, they must be more accountable for marketing efforts and costs.

It is in this context that Consumer Products, Inc. is experimenting to learn the value of database marketing applications in what has traditionally been a mass marketing arena.

Database Marketing Overview

Consumer Products, Inc. sees the power of personal communications with consumers as a customer acquisition tool more than as a customer relationship and lifetime value resource. Thus, the company's goals for database marketing are as follows:

- Identify and promote to consumers using competing products in our categories,
- Convert trials and low-frequency customers to increased purchase frequency, and
- Cross sell one-category purchasers to other categories.

Database Marketing Process

Consumer Products, Inc. has massive promotional power in the marketplace. With more than 100 brands couponing several times per year, the company has collected a large volume of customer data. The problem is that the data is spread over 15 promotion vendors across the country. The first step in the database marketing process was to consolidate the data for current and past promotions to a single location at an outside service bureau. The consolidated database took five months to build. Most of the time spent was coordinating, formatting, and identifying incoming data from 15 different sources.

The result was a database of more than 20 million households, tracking more than three years of promotional data for more than 60 brands. The database was maintained in a flat file format on a mainframe computer and was batch updated on a quarterly basis. Information was generated via hard copy reports and file extracts pulled from the database for analysis at the client location.

In addition to promotional responses, the company was committed to surveying consumers on their buying habits to gather customer and non-customer data. Consumer Products, Inc. mailed more than 30 million questionnaires asking about product and brand usage over a number of brand categories. Questionnaires were sponsored by a brand. Questionnaire responses were loaded into the database.

Database applications consisted of mailings and sampling programs. Mailings were primary solo. A brand would decide to mail to survey or promotion respondents or to both. The service bureau would then select a list for mailing. Sampling was conducted in the same manner. Because the coupon and sampling programs required "response" to go through retail and coupon redemption processing, results lagged by more than six months and were never accurate. Consumer Products, Inc. did not mail promotional programs with any customer relationship recognition at all. Thus, no prior purchase behavior was recognized even though it was tracked by the program.

Consumer Products, Inc. continues to invest in the capture and management of survey data and purchase-redemption data. However, programs have never been expanded to recognize the value of a customer relationship or purchase behavior over time.

Applications Analysis

Consumer Products, Inc. is classified as using a historical data management system.

Figure 5-3

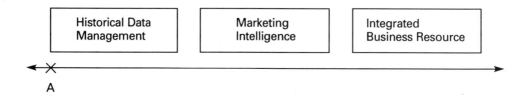

Only two of the three building blocks of database marketing are utilized in this application: data and technology. The company has made an effort to collect important and relevant data on customers and prospects. However, the applications generated from the file are not based on any level of segmentation or modeling. No effort has been made to develop customer relationships over time, to acknowledge existing relationships or encourage loyalty.

While this application is wide reaching, it is certainly not sophisticated. Consumer Products, Inc. should be commended for capturing and maintaining data and starting out in database marketing. Remember, there is no bad application, only differing levels of sophistication. With the key building blocks of data and technology in place, Consumer Products, Inc. is in position to expand its applications and database sophistication.

B. Big Picture Company

Business Profile

Big Picture Company produces and distributes major budget motion pictures, television programming, and other entertainment-related products via movie theaters, video cassettes, retail, and other vehicles. The company produces more than 50 movies per year, of which seven to ten are considered blockbuster quality. Major motion pictures and resulting theater revenue represent the largest revenue source for Big Picture Company.

Marketing Overview

Big Picture Company faces significant competition for share of consumers at movie theaters. Not only must the company predict consumer interests, it must fight against at least five other major film developers and other independent producers. Point-of-viewing is also a major area of concern. Theaters must convince retailers to carry and promote major films. Super theaters often offer consumers as many as five to eight film choices at a time, and viewing prices are constantly increasing to the point that many consumers are opting for cable or rental video cassettes instead of first-run movies.

To compete, film studios are forced to increase merchandising support for high-budget movies, lowering margins further and decreasing profits. Major producers such as Big Picture Company are looking for ways to increase consumer viewing of their first-run movies and loyalty to their studio's movies. They must also promote peripheral product sales, such as merchandise tie-ins and video cassettes.

Database Marketing Objectives

Big Picture Company designed a test to attempt to identify viewers of their first-run major motion pictures and create an ongoing relationship with viewers. The objective was to increase both theater sales and after-market product sales. The focus of the test was to determine the profitability of this effort on an ongoing basis.

Priorities of the test were as follows:

1. Identify frequent first-run movie viewers,

2. Establish gender/interests of viewers,

3. Create a relationship program to profitably increase viewer frequency of Big Picture Company releases.

Database Marketing Process

Since there is no readily available list of first-run movie viewers, Big Picture Company decided to pick of group of five multi-screen theaters showing their major releases in three diverse markets, and thereby identify viewers themselves. The identified viewers would then be enrolled in a relationship-marketing program.

To identify the theater viewers, Big Picture hired contractors who mounted video cameras on the front bumpers of their cars. The cars swept theater lots before picture showings and recorded license plate numbers. This process was conducted at all five theaters in the three markets for six weeks for all time-slots where Big Picture movies were showing.

The license plates recorded via video were key entered and then merge/purged to create a clean file establishing single and multiple event viewers by theater for each market. The license plate numbers were then matched against the various state DMV records provided by list compilers.

Once matched with name and address, the file was enhanced with household demographics and stored on mainframe computer in a flat file format with name, address, household demographics, and movie viewership and frequency, if captured.

Big Picture then developed a monthly communications program that informed viewers of upcoming movies, offered viewer incentives and advance screenings, and provided movie trivia. Preliminary analysis indicated that the relationship program increased viewer frequency. No profitability information is available on the application to date. To the best of our knowledge, the program has not been repeated.

Applications Analysis

Big Picture Company's database marketing application falls into the category of historical database management.

Figure 5-4

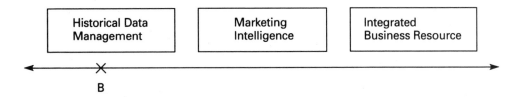

The application takes customer information and provides that data for communications programs. The results are tracked and managed in the database. Of the three key building blocks—data, technology, and statistical technique—data gathering is the most sophisticated. The custom development of theater customers and data enhancement to create a customer file was very creative. The technology used in the application was mainframe, off-line, batch-update processing. All reports were hard copy. No research or segmentation techniques were employed. On the continuum, the application is a sophisticated use of historical data management due to the creative data capture process.

C. *Read Me* Magazine

Business Profile

Read Me is a news magazine. It presents important news and information stories on issues of national and social importance. Revenues are generated from consumer subscriptions and advertising.

Marketing Overview

Read Me competes against an array of competitors. Its major problem is that news has become available as it happens. International and national broadcast networks provide on-the-spot, real-time coverage of any event anywhere in the world. Newspapers provide timely coverage of events.

Like other news magazines, *Read Me* has traditionally been able to differentiate its product from these media by providing in-depth coverage with more substance than real-time or next-day media. However *Read Me* has, in addition, three major competitors providing a similar product to consumers and competing for consumer subscriptions and advertising. There is also a new trend in magazine publishing towards providing customized or selective publishing to advertisers.

Database Marketing Objectives

Read Me has observed the current trend of niche marketing among consumer publications. Surveys also indicate that readers are interested in different features of the publication. *Read Me* conducted a study of subscription readers and asked them to "rebuild" the magazine to meet their information needs. The results of the study indicated that *Read Me* could create five subsegments or niches of the publication that would appeal more to large subsets of subscribers than a single, generic news magazine attempting to meet all subscriber needs. The study indicated that a generic version could be continued for subscribers on whom no data was available and for newsstand sales. Discussions with advertisers indicated that the niche versions offered the ability to target communications more effectively to subscribers.

The objectives of the marketing database test were to build on existing subscription data and to track subscriber information requirements. From the database, the magazine company planned to develop the appropriate sub-versions of *Read Me* and track the effectiveness of the activity.

Database Marketing Process

Read Me already had the beginning of a marketing database. Subscription information was managed by a third-party resource specializing in subscription database and overlayed it with demographic data. A test segment was selected for research purposes. The test segment was surveyed via several techniques to determine information and readership interests. Results generated the opportunity to create five subsegments or niche versions based upon customer profiles, interests, and information requirements. The niche versions extended to information and resources beyond the traditional news magazine that would be helpful to the subscriber. For example, if one segment was made of frequent travelers, the value-added would center around helpful travel- and business-related information. *Read Me* argued that the five subsegments went beyond providing news coverage to providing a relationship that gave relevant information to subscribers.

The publication tested the concept on two of the five niches to subscribers representing about five percent of total subscriptions. Subscribers were measured on readership, interest and renewal.

Applications Analysis

Read Me's database marketing application is classified as historical data management.

Figure 5-5

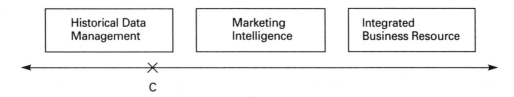

The application uses simple mainframe, batch-mode, hard-copy technology to manage data. The information developed is generated primarily from customer source data. The research functions proved to be the most sophisticated part of the application. Once customer-niche models were developed, the database was scored to identify all subscribers by their potential niche. *Read Me* did not include a strong feedback loop into the program that updated the database with the effectiveness of the effort. Decisions on program effectiveness were made based upon traditional research studies. *Read Me* developed the basis for a successful database marketing application, but did not develop the relationship/feedback with the customer the company hoped would develop based upon the niches. The application is plotted close to a marketing intelligence application, based upon the sophisticated use of data and research, but falls short because there is no feedback vehicle to provide ongoing intelligence to the database.

D. Beans & Brew

Business Profile

Beans & Brew is a retailer of coffee beans, tea, spices, and coffee drinks in a suburb of a large city. The owner of Beans & Brew is active in the business and employs four part-time employees at one location.

Marketing Overview

Beans & Brew provides gourmet products to upscale and discriminating consumers. Most customers live within a three-mile radius of the store. Many are regulars, and often stop in for a cup of Caffe Latte or Expresso and buy some beans. The owner knows many customers personally. Currently, there is no specialty retail competition in the immediate area. Specialty products are sold by local grocers. A national whole bean/coffee drink competitor has located two franchised stores in the nearby major metropolitan area.

Database Marketing Objectives

Develop relationship marketing programs with customers and manage frequency purchase program. In addition, Beans & Brew wants to develop new customers and test whether a mail-order program would take away from retail sales.

Database Marketing Process

The owner of Beans & Brew purchased a PC and list management software from a local computer store. He then started to collect name/address and purchase behavior information by hand from all customers. He updated his database himself on weekends. By the end of six months, he had collected records on 700 customers. Many had purchased more than six times.

Beans & Brew then conducted an analysis of customers and built three profiles. The first profile was of the average retail customer based upon geography and socio-economic indicators. The second profile was of good customers defined as three-time or more purchasers over a one-year period. The third profile was intended to look at *all* customers with the objective of generating a test list for a mail-order whole beans business.

The retail purchaser model was used to create mailings to expand retail sales. A series of three mailings were targeted to like-profile consumers around the store area who had not shopped there. This generated an initial increase of 35 percent in retail traffic and 80 percent in follow-up to customers who first visited the store as a result of the direct mail program. The computer generated a selection of customers who had obtained three or more purchases for special frequent-customer mailings, promotions, and events.

Beans & Brew also managed its frequent-purchaser program on the computer system. Based upon the retail purchaser profile, the owner bought a list of 100,000 names for a mail-order test. The initial mailing was conducted in a newsletter format. The order rate was eight percent, with an average order size of $12.00. Results of the test far exceeded the owner's anticipation. While ongoing mailings did not deliver the same results, Beans & Brew has developed a successful mail-order business. The synergy of both related businesses creates better buying power and even revenue flow.

Beans & Brew is now using its database power to help identify the location for a second store.

Applications Analysis

Beans & Brew is defined as a marketing intelligence system.

Figure 5-6

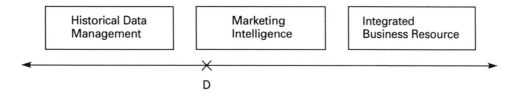

The owner of the company has integrated the three key building blocks—data, technology, and statistical techniques—to develop a successful system. Through data capture and analysis, Beans & Brew has been able to segment customers, develop targeted programs, develop multiple distribution systems, identify new customers, and successfully expand its retail business.

E. Smart Politician

Business Profile

You may think that the words "smart" and "politician" constitute an oxymoron, but what the heck. In this case, the politician is a 32-year-old MBA who ran for State Representative in a midwest state.

Marketing Overview

Politics, like most other businesses, is competitive. Our politician faced down three opponents in a primary election and won on new ideas, looks, brains, and youth . . . go figure. However, the general election was another story. He had enough brains to realize that the same attributes that gave him an edge over his primary opponents were matched by his general election counterpart. He was also convinced that he had a story to sell, but had to do it without spending a lot of money. He knew that he could generate a "list" of the electorate in his district, and he understood that direct mail could reach each home in the district.

Database Marketing Objectives

The objectives of our politician were to build a database of all the electorate in his district that would allow him to do two things:

1. Communicate based upon the unique needs of constituents,
2. Track interaction with constituents.

Database Marketing Process

Smart Politician purchased a list from his political party of all voters in his district. He then contracted with a local lettershop to manage it on PC. Then, along with a friend who was a researcher, he mailed a detailed survey on voters' issues and concerns in his district. He supplemented the mail return with one-on-one interviews throughout the district.

The survey results were then analyzed and the issues/concerns of his district clustered into six distinct groups that were trackable to unique socio-economic profiles of typical voters in the district. Based upon a census overlay, Smart Politician scored his voter file and segmented each household into one of six clusters. He validated the six clusters via telemarketing follow-up. In addition, whenever he went to a town hall meeting, a home meeting, or any kind of meeting in which he interacted with constituents, he tried to get the name and address of everyone he met.

Based upon the above, Smart Politician developed segmented communications to each voter based upon the election issues and their cluster, and overlayed a reminder of any personal contact he had with the voter. Over the course of the process, he continued to refine the clusters, statement of issues, and contact with each voter. By the end of the race, he had managed to extend personal contact to more than 70 voters based upon the ability to track his activity. He also had mailed personalized communications relevant to the election issues to all voters in his district at least five times. Some were mailed as many as eight times. All advertising was done via the database. He spent no money on mass media at all.

The results of the effort payed off. Smart Politician beat an incumbent from the opposing party by a margin of 65 to 35 percent. Our Smart Politician attributes his success to his ability to identify relevant issues, communicate accordingly, and acknowledge his relationship and contact with the voters via his marketing database.

Applications Overview

Smart Politician's process is classified as a marketing intelligence system.

Figure 5-7

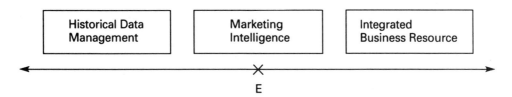

Via his PC, he was able to generate a basic file of all voters. Using a census overlay and custom-data development, he was able to build a segmentation structure that allowed relevant communications with voters. By capturing voter contact information (similar to purchase behavior in a consumer database), he was able to create a sense of relationship with the voter that went beyond the election issues. Both became very powerful political tools available to him because of a marketing database.

F. Hardware & Things

Business Profile

Hardware & Things owns and operates 110 retail discount do-it-yourself hardware stores across the United States. Each store provides an array of products and services from nuts and bolts to electrical, lumber, and plumbing supplies, and a variety of in-home services such as fence, bathroom and plumbing installations. Hardware & Things also services a large percentage of the contractors and building and repair trades near their locations. Contractors and trades are provided special services and resources in-store.

Marketing Overview

An analysis of sales indicated that trades and contractors represented only 20 percent of in-store traffic but 80 percent of an average retail store's revenue. This target audience also is the most competitive. Hardware & Things faces seven national and many local competitors all wooing the same contractor and trade audience on a store-by-store basis.

Database Marketing Objectives

Hardware & Things decided to develop a national, regional, and local database tracking trades and contractors and increase the array of in-store services based upon the target's purchase behavior and frequency. The database would also be used to create a relationship marketing program and feedback system. Specific objectives include:

- Capture and tracking of purchase behavior of existing trades,
- Development of programs to maintain and increase trades sales,
- Identification of trades that are not current customers,
- Marketing intelligence on trades purchase, price and promotion behavior.

Database Marketing Process

Hardware & Things contracted with a computer service bureau to develop and manage a comprehensive database of trades customers and prospects. The first step was to develop a point-of-sale customer and sales data-capture system. A separate register/point-of-sale counter was set up exclusively for trades sales. Signage encouraged all tradespeople to use this checkout procedure. Each contractor/company was signed up into the program and issued plastic cards for the company and each purchasing employee that would automatically give a five percent discount at the register on all purchases. Hardware & Things also developed a proprietary credit card for the use of trades and general consumers. The program registration and credit card served as the basis for the database. The registration card also requested the number of any third-party card also used by the tradesbuyer.

Point-of-sale data capture was accomplished in several manners. First, if a tradesbuyer used a credit card, the number, along with purchases, was matched to the existing credit card number on the database. New buyers, not yet on the database, were reverse-appended with name/address information. Second, if cash was used, the ID card number was captured and matched back to a unique code on each customer record on the database. Third, if a check was used, the check was copied and matched back to the purchase data. Customer data was key entered from the check and matched to customer data on the database. This would then update the record or identify new customers.

Each store uploaded point-of-sale information (both hard copy and data) to a central resource each night. The data was then coded by store and region, checks were key entered and matched to purchase data. On a weekly basis, the data was shipped to the service bureau.

The database was maintained in an off-line, flat-file format on main-frame. Reports were generated via hard copy on a weekly basis in a standard series and custom requests on an as-requested basis. Customer name/address information was matched against a business-to-business database on a regular basis to identify non-database trades in the local store area by type of trade specialty (i.e., painting, plumbing, etc.).

With this accomplished, Hardware & Things had developed a comprehensive database capturing over 90 percent of all trades purchasing at its branches. By matching against non-customer trades, Hardware & Things was able to identify an additional 30 to 50 percent increase in target audience by store. The database allowed the company to develop the following programs:

- Each existing trades customer was tracked by specialty area and measured by recency, frequency, sales volume, multi-branch use, and number of employees purchasing. Each database customer was ranked by the above criteria.

- Targeted communications were mailed based on purchasing behavior. Promotional discounts were matched to purchase behavior.

- A frequency program was developed to reward frequency via points redeemable for product and local events.

- A relationship marketing program was developed to offer value-added, such as special shopping hours, seminars, etc.

- New customers were effectively solicited based upon success with the database program.

- Hardware & Things generated valuable intelligence on the purchasing dynamics and behavior of the target audience.

Overall, the database program generated an increase of as much as 40 percent in some markets from existing customers. New customer sales increased by 80 percent, compared to time segments prior to the development of the database. Customer churn dropped by over 50 percent. Hardware & Things was able to adjust product mix and pricing strategies based upon the intelligence gained through the database.

Applications Analysis

Hardware & Things' process is classified as a marketing intelligence system.

Figure 5-8

This program takes advantage of all three key building blocks: data, technology, and statistical technique. While the technology does not provide on-line access to information, it is not necessary for the successful implementation of this application. The key to success was painstaking capture of information and segmentation of customers into subgroups for effective marketing programs. This program takes full advantage of tracking of customer purchase behavior to develop and improve programs. All communications are targeted based upon database information, and the results of communications programs are tracked.

G. WDBM Radio

Business Profile

WDBM is an FM-band radio station in a large midwest city. It offers a contemporary music format. There are three other FM and four AM stations in WDBM's ADI offering the same music format. There is a total of 12 FM and 16 AM stations in the market. WDBM is currently ranked the number two FM station in its format and the number four in terms of listenership in the market.

Marketing Profile

WDBM is in a very competitive marketplace. It is in constant competition with other stations both in and out of format for listenership. It is on the battle line every hour, each day. Winning the war for listeners and thus ratings is accomplished by perception (promotion), format, and substance (events and personalities). WDBM has strong drive-time personalities and good local presence to do third-party tie-ins and local events.

Database Marketing Objectives

Traditionally, listeners are treated as nameless faces on the other side of the microphone. However, the progressive general manager of WDBM believed that by database marketing, the station could reinforce listener loyalty via target marketing and thereby increase overall audience share.

Specific database marketing objectives are:

- Learn who customers are besides ADI tracking numbers,
- Market more effectively,
- Create loyalty,
- Dominate market share,
- Maximize potential of relationship and event programs,
- Increase tools available for advertisers.

Database Marketing Process

WDBM developed a sophisticated data capture and management program. The station developed on-air promotions each week, designed to gather write-in or call-in names capture. WDBM increased the frequency and scope of special events and third-party tie-in programs and developed a names capture mechanism for each event. A WDBM proprietary magazine and a line of merchandise for sale were also developed. All possible contacts were recorded and a frequency marketing program developed that rewarded listeners based upon a weighting structure assigned to various types of possible contact with the station. WDBM also developed ADI-wide surveys delivered by FSI, events, and third-party programs to capture names, addresses, and music interests of as many listeners as possible in the ADI. Once data was consolidated from all sources, external census, household demographics and syndicated cluster data were overlayed to provide a detailed picture of station and market listeners.

The database, with over 340,000 listeners and potential listeners, was managed on a mainframe at the station. There was PC access to data for the following:

- Customer analysis
  - event attendance
  - on-air promotions
  - magazine circulation/promotion
  - merchandise sales
  - frequency programs
- Promotion planning
- Research
  - customer tracking
  - competitive tracking
  - sweeps monitoring
  - program/event tracking
  - promotion tracking
- Advertising support

With the database, the station was able to identify its loyal-listener segment. Loyalty programs targeted to this audience were the magazine, merchandise and record sales, frequency-marketing programs and relationship/dialog programs designed to refine format and promotion programs.

With the names identified via survey of competitive station listeners and loyal WDBM listener profiles, the station was able to profile its target audience. The station was then able to develop listener acquisition programs and effectively track the result. WDBM could also directly contact loyal, switcher, and competitive listeners before ratings sweeps to promote current promotions. The station further promoted to listeners of other formats to switch during rating and promotional periods.

The database also provided advertisers to the station with three important options beyond air time. First, marketing via the WDBM magazine; second, a list of WDBM loyals, switchers, competitive customers, and other format competitive listener coverage; and third, detailed demographics and buying habits on WDBM coverage, beyond any other station's ability.

The program has proven very successful. WDBM has become the number one ranked FM station in format and the number two ranked FM station for overall listenership. Advertising revenues are climbing by over 34 percent and the database is growing by 20,000 to 30,000 names per quarter. Database management costs are offset by database-generated revenue opportunities, such as the magazine and merchandise sales.

Applications Analysis

WDBM Radio's process is ranked as an integrated business resource.

Figure 5-9

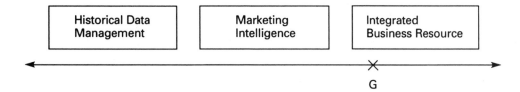

The strong use of source-data strategy to generate names of listeners, switchers, competitive listeners, and other station listeners was aggressive and strategic. Research techniques allowed the station to profile customers and effectively target new listeners. PC access to data in-house allowed the marketer to have direct access to information on a timely basis to make decisions.

H. Slots & More

Business Profile

Slots & More is a full-service, major casino in a Nevada city. It provides gambling, lodging, entertainment, food, and shopping to customers. Customers come for the day, stay at the hotel/casino, or stay at other locations in the area.

Marketing Overview

Slots & More competes against 15 major full-service casinos in its local area. In addition, it competes against more than 30 gambling-only locations. Competition is intense for gamblers, both casual and serious. The major casinos all market to the same audiences across the United States. Slots & More determined that it could maximize the information already gathered on customers to develop a sophisticated database marketing program.

Database Marketing Objectives

Casinos track everything. In fact, they even have a debit card to put in the slots that eliminates the need for silver. When you get home, you get a summary and bill. They track the gaming you play, the shows you attend, and almost every other activity you engage in at the casino. Slots & Things had access to this data, but it was not linked into one comprehensive system for customer and prospect marketing. Slots & More wanted to accomplish the following database marketing objectives:

- Identify all activities/services customers use during a stay,
- Track frequency of customer visits,
- Increase per-visit expenditures at facilities of Slots & More,
- Increase frequency of gambling/lodging visits to Slots & More,
- Identify non-customer gamblers and convert them to Slots & More customers.

Database Marketing Process

Slots & More has at least four non-interacting systems that track various aspects of customer activity. The reservations system tracks lodging and hotel meals, a second system tracks shows and events, a third tracks Slots & More and franchised store merchandise sales, and a fourth tracks casino activity for rated players. Slots & More hired a director of database marketing to focus on consolidating this activity.

A service bureau was hired to consolidate on a weekly basis the data flow from all four systems. The bureau created one master record for each customer on a mainframe computer with relational software. Each customer "event" or Slots & More activity was recorded on the customer master record, along with the data of the event. If no match was identified, a new record was created. The appearance of additional guests per customer per visit was tracked, but never used. On a regular basis, the database was enhanced with additional external demographic and lifestyle data purchased for a year's use.

The casino added additional tracking devices based upon a unique code all lodging guests received when they checked in. Similar to an ID card, the number was requested at restaurants, shops, and shows. Guests were offered the opportunity to "get rated" at each gaming activity they participated in via the ID card.

This tracking vehicle, along with others already in place, gave Slots & More the ability to track all activity of their customers inside their facilities. In addition, they developed a survey to measure customer migration to other casinos, restaurants, and shows during their stay to determine the level of spending per guest they were losing to other nearby casinos and entertainment. With this data in place, the mainframe system provided 12 standard management reports per week on guest activity and frequency of activity.

Once a benchmark had been established, various marketing programs were established. They include:

1. Guest-acknowledgement project. Four weeks after a stay, a survey was sent to gain information about the customer's experience. Results were updated into the database.

2. Frequent-stay program. Guests were enrolled in a frequent-stay program, offering points redeemable for lodging, shows, and meals.

3. Priority status for future stays and gambling with special privileges. This program attempted to cross-sell and up-sell customers based upon past behavior. It also arranged classes on gambling, instruction, priority show seating, upgraded lodging, and free gifts.

4. Targeted promotion mailings. Generation of future lodging and gambling visits based upon past behavior.

5. Targeted prospecting based upon geographic, demographic, and lifestyle analysis of customer base.

6. Special programs. Development of special programs for unique segments of the database such as "high rollers," frequent entertainment users, and high merchandise purchasers. The database maintained special security for these segments, with limited access by casino and service-bureau personnel.

Slots & More also developed a survey of gambling tied into a sweepstakes offer, which was mailed and inserted in magazines in selected target markets. The program generated thousands of prospective lodging and gambling customers. The survey asked questions on gaming, show, lodging, and other entertainment-related behavior. This data was entered into the database. With this segment of the database, Slots & More developed targeted mailings to identified gamblers to increase both lodging and casino business.

Applications Analysis

Slots & More is classified as an integrated business resource.

Figure 5-10

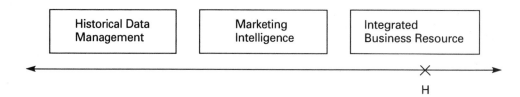

It maximizes the use of the three key building blocks of database marketing—data, technology, and statistical techniques. The source data strategy of Slots & More maximizes not only the ability to gather data internally, but uses custom data gathering techniques to gain data in a hard-to-find area. The use of marketing applications supported by relational technology and segmentation analysis and modeling generated new opportunities.

I. Mail Order Computers

Business Profile

If you pick up any computer magazine or major business publication, you cannot help but notice the major advertisements of a group of businesses that sell computers via mail order distribution only. Mail Order Computers is one of five major mail-order-only computer sales companies. The company has a line of eight PC systems, three laptop systems, and various peripherals.

Marketing Overview

The sales of PCs have grown very competitive. Competition forces prices downward and technology increases the array of add-ons and upgrades required to be competitive. Mail Order Computers actually assembles computers after orders are received. Thus, the assembly process changes for each order depending upon the nature of the PC to be assembled and delivered. Mail Order Computers needed to develop a system that would integrate all aspects of the business into a integrated business resource.

Database Marketing Objectives

The process of marketing and selling computers via mail order represents a number of processes that must be integrated into one system. A summary of the steps are as follows:

- Marketing promotions,
- Customer orders/service,
- Order entry/management,
- Order distribution to internal departments, such as accounting, assembly line, manufacturing, purchasing and marketing,
- Production,
- Quality control,
- Production follow-up, such as parts purchasing, shipping of product to customer, and accounting,
- Customer billing,
- Feedback to research, marketing, and manufacturing.

Mail Order Computers must develop a resource that will integrate all business resources together into one system.

Database Marketing Process

Mail Order Computers developed a full audit of all business requirements including data, data management, research, and all related processes. Each functional organization, such as marketing, provided a detailed proforma of required information, technology, analytical support, and integration requirements into the core resource. An outside consultant was hired to analyze the functional proformas and referee needs and requirements.

The result was a plan with process flow, data, technology, and inter-action requirements for the integrated system. The implementation of the system was handled with networked workstations manufactured by Mail Order Computers. Each functional area collected, reviewed, managed, analyzed and contributed relevant data that created an integrated resource for the company. Figure 5-11 is a flow chart of the integrated system and function integration.

Figure 5-11

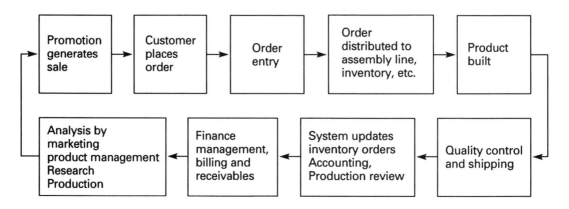

The role of marketing in the system is to contribute customer and prospect data to the customer and marketing database. Data is then extracted for promotion analysis and promotion planning. The promotion planning schedule updates inventory purchasing and production line scheduling processes. Finance triggers corporate analysis functions based upon sales/production flows.

For Mail Order Computers, the system allows each functional unit of the organization to manage its business function and, at the same time, keep a single core data resource that drives all functions. Mail Order Computers is operating a successful business on the lowest production and marketing margins in the industry, allowing the company to compete effectively on price/function against all competitors.

Applications Analysis

Mail Order Computers' system is a fully integrated business resource.

Figure 5-12

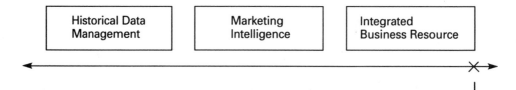

It transcends traditional marketing databases in that it maximizes the three key building blocks—data, technology and statistical technique—for all business functions, not just marketing. The requirements of each functional business unit (i.e., marketing, finance, assembly line, customer service, inventory/purchasing, distribution, research, etc.) is satisfied by access to any business-wide data accessed in the functional unit's PC based resource. However, all data provides intelligence to the overall business.

Compare Your Company to These Database Marketers

The nine cases we have presented run the range of database marketing applications. Large to small venture, sophisticated to basic, high technology to low, integrated and strategic to tactical. However, each has in common some use of the three key building blocks—data, technology, and statistical technique. There is no right or wrong application or program, only an opportunity to develop a powerful resource . . . if you do your homework. Hopefully you have gained some interesting insights by reviewing the case histories:

- Large volume and huge corporate resources do not necessarily lead to a sophisticated application. (Big is not always better.)
- Sophisticated technology (hardware/software and on-line access) is not a requirement for a successful database marketing program.
- Research does not necessarily have to be brain surgery. Simple segmentation may be all you need.
- Without the right data, nothing works.
- A database is a database, *but a marketing database requires a customer feedback mechanism or process.*

Learn all you can about the three key building blocks because they control the success of your marketing applications.

Part III of the book will allow you to focus on data and maximizing its value for *your* business. Part IV provides a non-technical discussion of technology. Part V focuses on statistical techniques. As you read each section, think of your database marketing application, these three building blocks, and your point of entry into database marketing.

Remember, even in the most basic examples we have presented in the chapter, the program was successful . . . even if the company was not. All of the marketers in the cases we talked to had fun doing it.

This book will provide the basics for you to build your own system and have some fun as well.

Happy building!

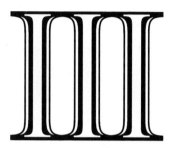

Three Key
Building Blocks
of a Database System:
Data, Technology, and
Statistical Techniques

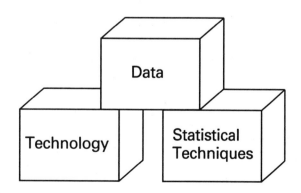

C H A P T E R   **6**

Data: A Database Is Only as Powerful as the Data It Houses

A database is only as powerful as the information it houses.

Jackson & Wang

As marketers, we can capture and maintain an amazing array of relevant information about our customers and prospects for target marketing purposes. And the data we gather is crucial in database marketing. A database is only as powerful as the information it houses. Think about that for a moment. Data is the most important key building block for data-driven marketing. You can build a technological masterpiece, have a staff of 40 statistical professionals and marketing gurus . . . but if you do not collect the right data, the other resources will never be used to their potential.

In this chapter, we will explore the relationship between communications or distribution channels and capturing information on customers and prospects; the concept of data enhancement; and the types and sources of data available to you as a database marketer.

The Database and Distribution Channels

To capture information about your customers or prospects, you have to learn who they are. In many cases, this means understanding the level of direct contact the marketer has with the consumer and the resulting role of the database as a home for information. In the simplified version of the distribution process displayed in Figure 6-1, we show four channels of distribution from the marketer or manufacturer to the consumer.

Figure 6-1   Multiple Distribution Channels

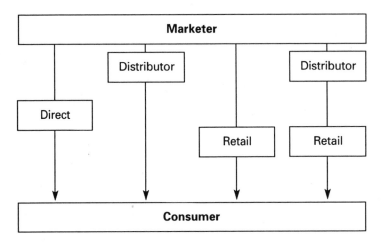

The channels range from direct distribution between the marketer and consumer to two intervening layers of distribution. Each distribution scenario involves different core issues. Each has unique communications issues with customers or distribution layers and each has access to a different level of information about the ultimate consumer.

Consider direct distribution from a marketer, for example a catalog marketer, to the consumer. The catalog marketer develops a product offering and communicates it directly to the consumer (Figure 6-2).

Figure 6-2

Via lists, the cataloger knows who has been targeted. The cataloger has established a direct seller-purchaser relationship with the consumer. As a by-product of this relationship and direct communications process, the cataloger can ask the consumer for information that will be relevant to targeting sales offers. The marketer can ask for this data via direct communications with the consumer. Information not available from other sources can be obtained, such as age, family size, lifestyle, and other relevant data for targeting a catalog of products.

At the other end of the scale, marketers with multiple layers of intervening distribution face different issues. They very seldom get the opportunity to talk directly to their consumer. This communications process is "short-stopped" by one or more layers that isolate the manufacturer from the consumer. Examples include almost any consumer product or service that is sold by an organization other than the manufacturer (Figure 6-3).

Figure 6-3

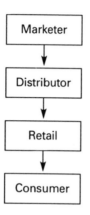

They range from dishwashing liquid to mutual funds. Typically, this creates two problems for marketers. First, they lose touch with the customer as an individual because the relationship is really between the retailer and consumer. Marketers in this predicament tend to view their customers as aggregate statistics because specific information is hard to gather. Second, where there are two or more intervening layers of distribution, the manufacturer may not even know the name of the retailer that sells his products. Many distributors keep the retailers secret from the manufacturer so they can keep control of the distribution process.

Data-driven marketing programs allow marketers in intervening distribution environments to capture valuable data on who their customers are and even who is selling their products. A manufacturer of air conditioners and refrigerators sells product to a distributor who remarkets it to hundreds of independent electronics retailers around the country. Until database marketing tactics were available, this marketer often learned of new retailers by looking at the yellow pages. Talking to the consumer was limited to focus groups and customer complaints. Via data-driven marketing and a data development strategy, the manufacturer can capture a great deal of information on customers and retailers, and in turn develop better programs to support both. Another example comes from financial services.

A marketer of several mutual funds sold via brokers really has no relationship with the consumer. They have been forced to view the broker as the customer. By developing a data-driven marketing strategy, the fund developer can track and communicate with consumers and at the same time, track and communicate with the consumers' brokers.

Data Enhancement: What It Is and How to Use It

No matter what distribution environment you market into, a database becomes your information and intelligence resource. Core to maximizing the information in your database is the ability to add outside data to create enhanced information on your customers. Data enhancement has been one of the hot topics of database marketing for several years. However, as with the word *database,* data enhancement means different things to different marketers. The interest in data enhancement is related to the almost limitless amount of information available about most consumers as individuals or households. If used correctly, this wealth of available information can be a major tool to help develop a list or database into a valuable information resource.

Database enhancement is defined as the overlay of information to customer or prospect records for the purpose of better describing or better determining the responsiveness of the customers or prospects. There is a tendency to get carried away with the appending of a file or database with outside data. However, the process of data enhancement is never the goal, but rather the means to the end. There are three primary reasons to enhance a database. They are to learn more about customers or prospects, to increase the effectiveness of customer programs, and to predict responsiveness for prospecting programs.

To Learn More about Customers

By learning more about who buys your products and services, you can adjust all the strategic functions of a business from marketing, through distribution, through development. Usually, data developed internally is limited to the purchase of a product or service. With relevant external data overlayed on customer data, a marketer can gain a valuable picture of customers by their value to the marketer. This picture can contain demographic, lifestyle, and behavioral data. The data is developed into a customer profile that allows the marketer to distinguish different customer groupings in the database by more than product purchases.

To Increase the Effectiveness of Customer Programs

By learning more about good customers, you can understand how to maximize customer communications and cross-sell opportunities. Through the development of customer profiles, a marketer can gain insight into customer propensity for additional and other product purchases. This could not be accomplished without external data overlayed on each customer record so that customers could be compared and analyzed by characteristics such as demographics and psychographics in addition to product purchases.

To Predict Responsiveness for Prospecting Programs

By understanding the target profiles of best customers, you can find prospects who match that profile and increase the probability of success for new sales programs. Overlay of external data allows an "apples-to-apples" comparison of outside lists by common characteristics such as demographics that would not be available in customer databases without data enhancement.

The Three Dimensions of Enhancement Data

The data available for database enhancement can be categorized into three interacting dimensions, geo-unit, target, and attributes.

Figure 6-4 Three Dimensions of Enhancement Data

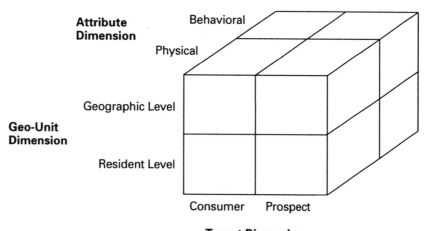

Target Dimension

The geo-unit dimension categorizes the geographic levels available for data selection. The most valuable data available for database enhancement is generally sourced at one of two levels—resident or geographic. At the resident level, information is appended to database records by individual (first name and surname) or by household (surname only). The geographic level provides information at a higher geographic level such as block group, carrier route, or zip code. Data at this level cannot be recognized as being from a specific household, but represents an aggregate of the households in the geographic area, such as census data.

The target dimension describes whether the records in the database are customers or noncustomers. Customer files generally include proprietary information such as sales by product, dollar amount, and payment type. In many cases, customer information can be analyzed on its own with limited overlay data required compared to analysis of noncustomer data.

The attribute dimension is also broken down into two categories—behavioral and attitudinal data. Behavioral data describes the demographic characteristics of a household or individual. Examples include demographics such as age, income, family size, car type, and occupation. Attitudinal data describes the factors that make the behavior of two demographically similar households different. Examples include leisure interests, financial and purchasing patterns, product purchases, and beliefs.

The Dynamics of Enhancement Data

The availability of data within each dimension affects the combination of information that can be overlaid for data enhancement. The geo-unit and target dimensions are called *prequalifying* or *driver* dimensions because the types of data available in these dimensions predetermines the type and level of data that can be overlaid from the attribute dimension.

The dynamic nature of the interaction among the three data dimensions is expressed by the following example. Company X maintains a database of customers. New customers are developed primarily through print and television advertising efforts. Company X wants to develop direct mail as a new prospecting tool. Analysis of resident data in the customer database proved useful for segmentation for offer development. However, it provided no information that would transfer to targeting of outside lists for prospecting. External demographic and leisure interest data was therefore overlaid on the customer database to develop customer profiles that matched outside lists.

The resulting analysis showed few distinguishing characteristics based upon demographics, but several lifestyle or leisure characteristics that were present in the customer file in percentages much greater than in the general population. The lifestyle data proved predictive for new customer development, but was available in outside lists only in limited quantity at the resident or individual level and in greater quantity when summarized to higher levels of geography such as carrier route.

In this example, both the geo-unit and target dimensions were driver dimensions. Sufficient data did not exist to develop prospecting profiles from the customer database, thus, both customer and noncustomer target classifications prequalified the choice of data in the attribute dimension. The geo-unit dimension proved also to prequalify the attribute data because limited data was available at the geo-unit resident level. Within the attribute dimension, behavioral data proved nonpredictive, while attitude-related data distinguished the customer from the general population. The interaction of the levels and types of data within the three dimensions thus determined data enhancement requirements unique to the marketing situation.

The reality of data enhancement falls somewhere between the two extremes of technical formulas and merely slapping some data on a database. The answer for your business lies in understanding your customers and database. But most important, the building block of data will not work without the building block of statistical analysis. The preceding description of data enhancement is meant to illustrate the complexity of data relationships. It is important for the marketer to appreciate the dynamic nature of data enhancement when applied to a database and the ramifications of the data enhancement process on your data-driven marketing efforts.

Where Does the Data Come From?

Part of our initial definition of a database was as a comprehensive collection of interrelated data. This data may come from customer files, order and return records, service reports, application forms, enhancement data, market research, prospect files, and many other sources. In general, there are two basic ways to put data into your database. First, you can develop data from your relationship with your customer or prospect and second, you can purchase data from an external source for database enhancement.

Internal Data Sources

Data that you collect about your customers or prospects is limited by your access to your targets and by the willingness of the customer or prospect to give you the information. In the next chapter we will discuss a strategy to maximize the data that you can collect from your customers. The following are examples of internally developed consumer data elements:

Customer identification number assigned by marketer

Name

Title

Address (may include a primary and secondary address such as a business and home address)

Sex

Age

Income

Length of residence

Size of household

Single or multiple residence

Acquisition source

Acquisition date

Telephone number

Order method (catalog/telephone)

Distance from retail store

Do not mail

Offer exposure

Offer response

Purchase history

Lifestyle data

Predictive score or customer value

Source of order

Amount of transaction

Payment method (check, credit card)

Product category

Style

Mailing code

Mailing date

Some business-to-business database characteristics include:

Identification number

Company name

Buyer's name

Buyer's title

Influencer name

Influencer title

Address (multiple addresses)

Telephone number

Industry classification (SIC)

Business size: revenue, number of employees

Anticipated demand for our products

Channels used for ordering

Offer exposure

Offer response

Purchase history

Predictive scores

Because each marketer has its own unique data requirements, the information that you will need to capture will vary for your business. This list is representative of the types of information you can capture and maintain. Many other elements could be added that marketers are capturing about their customers.

External Data Enhancement Sources

Many resources are available from which a marketer can purchase external data for overlay onto your own database. Generally, this data falls into three broad categories. They are compiled data, behavioral data, and modeled data.

Compiled Data.

The first category of external data, compiled data, represents an array of information that is gathered by data providers about consumers and businesses. The most used sources of consumer compiled data are demographic databases. Compiled by companies including Donnelley Marketing, Metromail, and R. L. Polk, these databases are combinations of several sources to create databases of demographics on almost all United States households. Generally these databases start with public data such as driver's license, auto registration, and white pages telephone directories to develop a base list. Additional data sources are added to provide a great depth about each household. Examples of data available include:

Name/address/telephone number

Home ownership

Sex of head of household

Number of residences at address

Length of residence

Number of adults present

Number of children present

Names and ages of family members

Income

Occupation

Marital status

Make of cars owned

Other organizations including Donnelley Marketing, and National Demographics and Lifestyles compile consumer lifestyle and leisure activity data obtained directly from the consumer. Examples of lifestyle data include:

Interest in book reading

Interest in bicycling

Interest in cable television

Interest in crafts

Interest in electronics

Interest in fishing

Interest in golf

Interest in pets

Interest in running

Interest in snow skiing

Interest in wines

Yet more data is collected by the federal government via the U.S. census. This data is remarketed by companies including Donnelley Marketing, Metromail, and R. L. Polk. Census data is not available on individuals, but on small areas of geography such as census tract or block group. Examples of census data include:

Households with income of $30,000 or more

Households with children

Adults age 18–24

With home value greater than $50,000

Adults with some college

Housing units in single-unit structures

Dwellings built between 1960–1969

One-person household

Moved in since 1975

Employed in agriculture

White

Federal workers

In college

Traveling 30 or more minutes to work

Other companies such as Dun & Bradstreet and American Business Information (ABI) collect demographic data on businesses. Examples available for purchase include:

Company name/address/telephone number

Standard industrial code (SIC)

Number of employees

Gross sales

Primary products produced

Branch locations

Name/title of key employees

Behavioral Data

The second type of external data, behavioral data, represents information collected about consumer financial, buying, and attitude patterns. Generally, this data must be observed and reported for the consumer or collected directly from the consumer. Examples include

Mail order buyers of products

Women's apparel

General merchandise

Crafts/sewing

Books/subscriptions

Health/fitness

Donors

Sweepstakes responders

Smokers

Credit card users

Purchasers of stocks and bonds

Oil and gas purchasers

Make/model of cars owned

Products purchased by category and source

Modeled Data

The third category of data available is modeled data. Organizations such as Microvision and Prizm collect individual- and census-level data to develop models of consumer purchase behavior that can be purchased to overlay on consumer databases. The concept implies that people with similar cultural backgrounds, means, and perspectives generally gravitate toward one another. They share similar patterns of consumer behavior toward products, services, media, and promotions. Various models have been developed that create between forty and fifty clusters that group all households into targeting groups. Examples of clusters include

Blue Blood Estates

Money and Brains

Furs and Station Wagons

Shotguns and Pickups

Upper Crust

Good Family Life

Successful Singles

Sunset Years

Bedrock America

All of the external enhancement data sources we have discussed are available for overlay on your customer database. Generally, you can negotiate to overlay this data on your database for a one-year period, and ownership of the data remains with the compiler. The cost for data overlay can be very high because most compilers of data spend a great deal of time and money to compile it and also market the same information as rental lists for mailers.

In the next chapter we will explore a strategy to maximize the use of this data in developing your own enhancement data.

C H A P T E R 7

Data: Developing a Source Data Strategy

Marketers . . . have assembled vast databases identifying their customers and their buying habits. With such information, companies now believe it's as important to reach the right people as it is to reach lots of people.

Business Week, September 23, 1991

A database is only as good as the information it contains. This is the basic premise of any type of database marketing system. If the information required to drive smart marketing decisions is not in the database, you cannot develop data-driven marketing programs.

The information contained in a marketing database is called *source data.* Source data in a marketing database can be as simple as customer name and address, or as complete as a record of every communication with a customer and a prediction of his or her actions in the future.

The range of information in between is up to your marketing requirements. . . .

Source Data Is the Heart of Database Marketing

It is important to remember not to get wrapped up in putting source data into your database as your ultimate goal. Data is simply a means to the end of data-driven marketing. Some marketers capture over 600 pieces of information on each customer, some only 10. Do not lose track of the fact that a marketing database is unique to each application. The amount of data that is relevant for your marketing situation may not be relevant for another marketing database.

Figure 7-1

Source Data
is the Heart
of Database
Marketing

Source data is so important to database marketing that we have developed a six-step strategy to maximize the relevant information that you keep in your database.

The six steps are

Step 1: Determine the value of data as a resource for your marketing database applications

Step 2: Evaluate and maximize your internal data-gathering resources

Step 3: Evaluate and maximize your external data-gathering resources

Step 4: Evaluate and maximize custom data development options

Step 5: Confirm the correct mix of source data for your database marketing applications

Step 6: Develop a corporate source data strategy for your marketing database

Step 1: Determine the Value of Data as a Resource for Your Marketing Database Applications

A database is both a marketing tool and a marketing information resource. The first step in the source data strategy is to determine the value of information that could be captured in a database for all the groups and applications that database might support in your organization. Why? First, the power of a marketing database increases with the relevant source data it contains. Second, the more business functions in a marketing organization share database applications and data, the more cost to develop a marketing database can be spread among the various users of the system.

What values does data have as a resource to your marketing and related functions? Some examples include advertising, sales, management information, research and development, brand management, customer service, order fulfillment, distribution, inventory, and finance.

Once you have considered the range of applications that meet your business requirements, evaluate the groups in your organization that might interact with the information. After you have identified the appropriate applications and functions, develop a data proforma.

Figure 7-2   Data/Applications Proforma

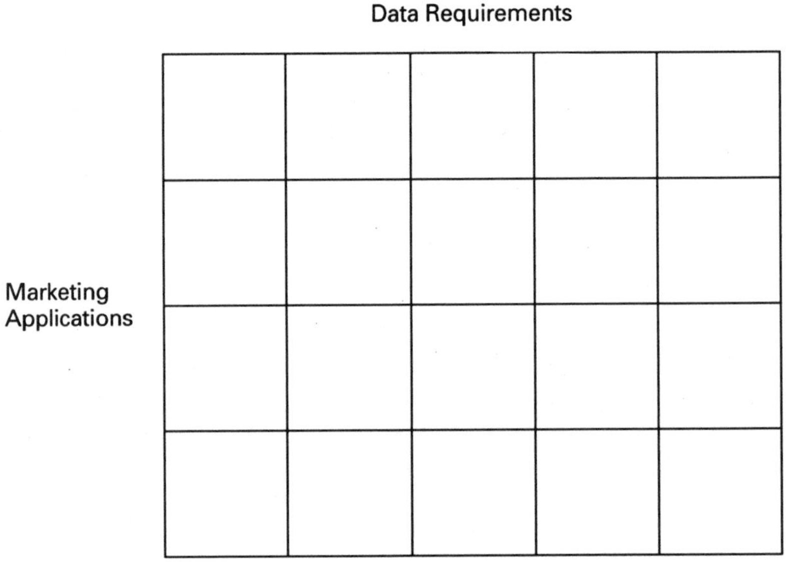

Data Requirements

Marketing
Applications

For the purposes of this proforma, let the sky be the limit for data desires. Ask each group to list all the data that they might need without regard to the cost of gathering and managing the information. At the end of this "wish-list" process, list all of the potential database uses in your data proforma. At this point, the same information may be required by various applications and functions, and some requests for data may seem beyond any true functional need.

Now, meet with each group and audit their information requirements in terms of their information needs. This process usually is a matter of common sense. Marketing requires both common business data and unique data to implement data-driven marketing applications. After the audit process, develop a revised list of data requirement if all groups and applications could have all the data they wish.

Step 2: Evaluate and Maximize Your Internal Data-Gathering Resources

Now you can review your data proforma in terms of the data that you can gather about your customers or prospects as part of your communications process with your customers. The information you will be able to gather depends on the level and type of access you have to your customers. Evaluate all the ways you currently communicate with your customers. There are probably more than you will first think of. Some communications methods are promotions, orders, customer service, service and repair, product queries, dealers and retailers, newsletters, warranty cards, billing, and returns, just to name a few. Compare your business functions to this list. You will probably also find several other customer communications options. The key is to be creative.

Recently a colleague purchased a product from a children's catalog. Via the 800 number, the order taker requested information on the number and ages of her children before asking for order information. Traditionally, catalog marketers have been some of the most conservative in changing the status quo of the customer communications process. They did not change anything that would damage the customer order lifeline. Clearly, for this example, the catalog marketer was willing to break from the mold. Now that they have our colleague's children's ages as well as the fact that she is now a customer, the cataloger will be able to create a relationship-driven communications program with her and her family.

An inverted triangle can be used to represent a marketing database and the types of source data it contains, as shown in Figure 7-3.

Figure 7-3   Source Data in a Marketing Database

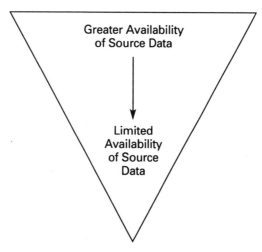

Greater Availability
of Source Data

Limited
Availability
of Source
Data

Within the triangle, the top or large end represents the largest sources of data in the database going down the triangle to the most limited sources of data.

Figure 7-4 is a model of a typical database with internal data sources represented and would have name and address data at the top of the triangle as the obvious largest source of customer data. The second largest data source is usually basic descriptive data that is collected as part of the communications process with the customer. This is followed by promotion and sales information and other distribution channel data. Each marketer will have a slightly different model of internal source data.

Figure 7-4   Internal Data Sources

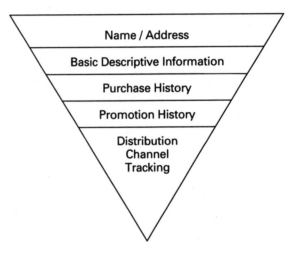

In a business-to-business source data model, as in the consumer model, the largest source of data would be business name and address, followed by company-level buying demographics. This data would include data that describes the company such as SIC code, sales volume, number of employees, and business activities. This is followed by the sales history of the marketer with the customer and then personal-level buying demographics. Personal-level buying demographics include names and titles and other relevant data (such as secretary's name, birthday, or characteristics) of the individuals who purchase and recommend purchase of products. At the bottom of the triangle, data sources would include competitors' sales and other proprietary data as tracked by your company. A business-to-business model is shown in Figure 7-5.

Figure 7-5   Business-to-Business Data Sources

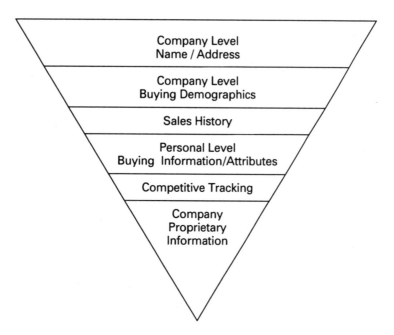

After you have identified all the realistic sources for development of source data internally, you need to ask several additional questions. The first is, What is my internal data shelf-life? For example, birth-date data lasts the prospect's lifetime. Addresses change, however—approximately 20 percent of all consumers move each year. Other demographics also change, such as number of children or car makes. The second question to ask is, What is my competition doing? Are they collecting any data as a part of the customer communications process that you are not collecting? If so, this is a pretty good indicator that you should examine reasons for collecting more data.

Now, compare the sources you have developed internally to your source data proforma from Step 1 and revise your source data proforma by eliminating the data that you can gather through internal sources. Then build an inverted-triangle source data model representing your internal data development process.

Step 3: Evaluate and Maximize Your External Data-Gathering Resources

External source data can come from many sources. In Chapter 5 we identified a sample selection of external source data suppliers and the types of data they offer. To recap, externally available business-to-business source data includes:

- Company demographics: SIC code, number of employees, sales volume, number of branches, key contacts
- Predictive complementary product information
- Competitive sales data
- Industry surveys
- Research
- Surveys of competitors
- Vertical publications for your industry
- Trade show lists
- Salesperson prospect and customer lists

Predictive complementary product information is data you may be able to collect about the purchase behavior of a customer or prospect that will indicate propensity to purchase your products or services. For example, if a company purchases a very heavy volume of copier paper, then it is highly likely that they have an ongoing need for copiers. Externally available consumer source data include:

- Demographic data
- Lifestyle/Leisure interests
- Financial characteristics
- Product purchase data
- Direct response data
- Promotional data

After you have reviewed all the relevant external source data options, revise your source data proforma by eliminating the data that you can gather through external data enhancement. In addition, build a revised inverted-triangle source data model reflecting both internal and external source data.

Step 4: Evaluate and Maximize Custom Data Development Options

If your source data proforma accomplished its objective, there are probably data elements on your wish list or proforma that have not been realized via internal or external source data development options. The only way to obtain this data is to be creative and develop your own source for this data. The following are some examples of custom source data development:

- Custom surveys
- Co-op surveys
- Research panels
- Customer participation promotions
- Warranty cards
- Relationship enhancement programs

Because of their distribution limitations and resulting limited communications options, many marketers develop custom programs to capture a great deal of relevant data about customers. Examples include cigarette companies, liquor companies, casinos, hotels, airlines, consumer products manufacturers, banks, and business-to-business marketers.

One of our favorite examples is the following. Casinos are probably the best at maximizing their internal source data capabilities. From the moment you check in, they attempt to track your every move. From trips to the restaurant and shows to physically tracking the better gamblers around the casino, they feed all the information back into their databases for future marketing programs. The best have frequent user programs and special credit/debit cards to track all your spending. They even have slot machine cards that keep track of your pulls on the lever and bill you at the end of the month. However, no matter how good they are at tracking your movements inside the casino, they cannot track you at other casinos or gain lists of prospects who are known to gamble. The only lists belong to other casinos, and they are not willing to share them.

Therefore, to create a prospect list, one Reno casino developed a sweepstakes promotion that ran as an insert in *TV Guide* in the northwestern United States. The promotion offered three winners the opportunity to design their own fantasy three-day, two-night getaway for two. The only requirement was that the entry questionnaire had to be filled out completely. First, they asked respondents to design their own weekend:

- How would you like to travel?

  auto, rental car, Amtrack, bus

  If your own car, how many miles will you drive? (the casino will reimburse mileage)

- What type of room would you like?

  suite, deluxe, king, or two double beds

- How do you prefer to dine?

  steak, seafood, dinner show, buffet, coffee shop, or room service

- What would you like to do in the area?

  health club, limo for shopping/sightseeing, rental car, skiing, golf, tennis, museums

Then they moved on to questions on gambling and Reno:

- Have you ever been to Reno? How often?
- What games do you play?

  slots, blackjack, craps, baccarat, poker, roulette, keno, race/sports books

- What is your gambling budget?
- Where do you stay when you come to Reno?
- How would you like your cash if you win?

  100s, 50s, 20s, 10s

- What do you earn yearly?

The promotion was very successful. Consider that the casino now has developed a promotional database of prospects that have identified themselves as gamblers, given their previous destinations, and discussed their gaming interests and budgets. This provides the casino the ability to develop the ultimate database marketing resource. It can understand, track, and communicate with customers based upon their relationship with the casino and develop a targeted universe of qualified prospects that can be marketed based upon the casino's products and market.

While developing custom data programs can become expensive, for many marketers, the benefits far outweigh the costs. Each organization will have to evaluate the uniqueness of the data to be collected, the size of the target audience, and the relevance to maximizing customer development programs in making the decision whether to develop a custom data source. For casinos, cigarette companies, hotels, consumer products marketers, banks, and many other marketers, the benefits of identifying competitors' customers via custom programs is becoming core to the marketing effort. They are in a war to take business from competitors. From their perspective, the investment pays out many times over with products purchased over time.

Step 5: Confirm the Correct Mix of Source Data for Your Database Marketing Applications

You now need to make the decision whether you will or will not capture or maintain the data identified in your proforma. Via internal, external, and custom development options, you have determined a means to develop all the data you identified as possibly useful for your data-driven marketing programs. Now it is time to further examine your data needs. It is great to have information on customers or prospects in your database, but this costs money, time, and effort. And someone in your organization is going to say, "this is great, but prove to me that this is worth the time, money, and effort," and they will be right to do so.

Because each data development effort has its own implications, you should test all aspects of each identified data development opportunity. Test expanding customer communications options via internal communications processes. Modify a test group of order forms. Test asking more telemarketing questions. Evaluate the impact of each option and related data element you can collect.

External data sources can be overlayed via data enhancement and evaluated for completeness and relevance in the communications process. Custom data development projects can also be tested for the amount and quality of information that you can develop for the cost.

After you have assessed the development impact, the real bottom line to your testing is to determine if the data provides relevant information for your data-driven marketing program. Did it allow you to:

- Learn more about your customers or market
- Develop better products
- Sell or cross-sell product
- Develop new customers
- Keep customers
- Distribute product more effectively

Or accomplish other worthwhile organizational goals? (Data evaluation techniques are discussed in detail in Chapters 9 and 10.)

After your analysis and data testing process, eliminate the data on your proforma that is probably not worth the cost required to gather it. Careful selection of the data you do choose to develop will go a long way toward allowing you to achieve your database marketing potential.

Step 6: Develop a Corporate Source Data Strategy for Your Marketing Database

Now that you have tested and evaluated the relevance of the data you intend to collect on customers and prospects, you can create a final data proforma. This final proforma should not only list the data sources and applications, but also rank each data development process by importance to your marketing effort and by cost. With this document, you can allocate your financial resources for data development to the areas that provide the most important impact to the company.

Given the value of data-driven marketing applications to multiple users in the business and the value of a database as a resource for your company, your own source data strategy must be viewed as a strategic resource. As such, the company must make a multiyear commitment to providing the data that has been identified as important. This commitment must translate into a long-term data acquisition plan.

Budget a multiyear program to accomplish the proforma data objectives. Start with the most critical data requirements and the data sources that will have direct and visible impact in the first year, and move to other data sources over a three- to five-year period. This process may seem to be an impossible task. However, you will be surprised how much data you can collect over a three- to five year period.

Figure 7-6   Data Coverage over Time

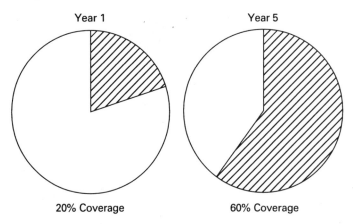

If you view this process strategically, you can set goals for both coverage and depth of data in your database. Coverage represents the overall number of records containing a key data element such as birth date. Depth represents the density of the coverage of required data elements in your database—in other words, the number of key elements contained in each individual record. Set realistic goals. For example, it is realistic if you have a corporate commitment to cover at least 20 percent of all records with key data elements during the first year of the data development process. By year five, you can have covered at least 60 percent of the records in the database with key elements.

Percentages of coverage and depth vary by data type, sources, and marketing requirements. For example, external data enhancement may cover at a 60 to 70 percent match rate. However, density of a single element inside an overall match rate may be significantly lower. That is because in all external databases, coverage of each element to be overlayed is not consistent between records. For example, one record may include birth date but not telephone number, while another includes telephone number but not birth date.

A Warning

As we have already warned, don't get trapped by the Great Database Marketing Paradox by neglecting to commit the resources necessary to use your database once you have acquired it. Data enhancement is one of the three key building blocks of database marketing. Your database marketing effort will not and cannot succeed unless you make a strategic commitment to developing the correct source data strategy for your marketing applications. It is all right if you cannot afford to obtain all the data necessary to implement a source data strategy in the first year. Start and do what you can. You will see, in the following case histories, that you can do a great deal on your own.

We feel so strongly about this point, that we recommend that you not attempt a database marketing effort if you are not going to commit to a source data development program. To fail to do so will almost guarantee failure. If necessary, wait and do it right at a later date.

Three Case Histories of Source Data Strategy

The process of development and implementation of a source data strategy can seem rather academic when simply illustrated as a six-step strategy.

We would like to present three case histories that represent a range of data-driven marketing applications and resulting source data strategies. The names and situations have been changed to protect the security of these very successful data-driven marketing programs.

Big Bank, Inc.: Using a Source Data Strategy to Maximize Customer Relationships

Big Bank, Inc. is a midwest banking company. They have over 30 branches spread out statewide, and many competitors at the state and local levels. Big Bank has four objectives for data-driven marketing:

1. Maximize product sales opportunities with existing customers
2. Cross-sell products
3. Develop new customers
4. Gain marketing intelligence

As they developed a marketing database, Big Bank conducted a data proforma. The following is their data "wish list":

- Customer name and address with a link to all accounts at the address
- Spouses' and children's names and ages
- Work and home addresses
- Financial potential ranking
- List of all current products in bank and link to other household members with products
- Products with competitive banks
- Key buying demographics such as income, home ownership, stocks and bonds, age, and family size

A review of internal data sources revealed the following information they could develop themselves:

- Branch/transaction data linked by multiple branch usage (work/ home) and by individual and household
- Credit cards held
- ATM usage
- Family demographic data (requested when the banking relationship is established)

External data sources could overlay the following data on Big Bank's database:

- Demographic data
- Financial characteristics
- Lifestyle/leisure interest data
- Overlay models of financial behavior

Custom data options include:

- Custom surveys of customers
- Promotions to generate targeted data items such as children's birthdays
- Telemarketing
- In-branch attempt to generate relevant data on a per-customer basis

Big Bank then tested all data development options. Internal data-gathering techniques were evaluated for potential, quantity, and customer complaint potential. The bank found that relevant data requests, when positioned correctly, were not objected to by customers. External data sources for demographics and financial overlay data proved valuable for modeling and profiling. Custom data options such as telemarketing, special promotions, and surveys generated substantial data at a lower cost than external data overlay. Based upon this analysis and testing, the bank developed a final data proforma ranked by application and immediacy of the impact of the data development effort. Data ranking was as follows:

1. Internal data consolidation to identify individuals by product linked to household
2. Demographic and financial data generated by all three sources for profiling and modeling
3. Competitive data development
4. All other data

Big Bank then developed a five-year data development plan to maximize the relevant demographic, financial, and competitive data in their databases. Year one efforts generated 40 percent coverage of most data characteristics. By year three, the bank had over 60 percent of customer records appended with the desired customer characteristics. Data-driven applications improved by the source data strategy included:

1. Customers ranked by potential

    By product

    Multiple products—The Bank could evaluate the customers who represented the greatest potential to the bank by revenue and multiple products, then identify households and individuals that meet the best customer profile.

    By household

2. Cross-sell—By identifying best customers by product, the bank could find customers in other product areas that matched the profile.

3. Relationship marketing

    Flag problems

    Identify customer changes (for example, changes in lifestyle or life stage)

4. Prospect identification

5. Marketing intelligence

    Customer base

    Market potential

    Product analysis

Cop-E-It Corporation: Using a Source Data Strategy to Maximize an Integrated Data-Driven Marketing Program

Cop-E-It Corporation is a small player in a big, competitive business category. They manufacture and market small document reproduction systems . . . a fancy name for photocopiers. Their major competitors include names such as Xerox, Kodak, and Canon. Cop-E-It is a business-to-business marketer selling to all SIC codes and businesses that need copiers. They focus on small, limited-volume business requirements. The purchase decision maker varies greatly by company, as does the decision-making process for a sale. They have a small national sales force of three good sales people and a trade sales force of twelve. As you can guess, Cope-E-It has a hard time competing against its much larger, financially stronger and larger line competitors.

Cop-E-It's management had determined that a data-driven targeting strategy was the only way for a small company to survive in a sea with much bigger fish. Cop-E-It's goals for data-driven marketing and source data development are as follows:

1. Maximize sales potential

2. Increase national accounts

3. Increase trade representation

4. Upsell and cross-sell existing accounts

5. Generate leads for the trade

6. Create a marketing information resource for better decision making

The following is the result of Cop-E-It's very extensive data proforma analysis:

- National account prospects

    Number of departments/locations

    Number of employees

    SIC/application

    Competitive sales/age of product

    Potential

    Key contact

- Trade prospects

    Sales volume

    Number of salespersons

    Territory coverage

    Competitive product lines

    Complementary product lines

    Key contact

- Copier prospects

    Number of departments/locations

    Number of employees

    SIC/application

    Competitive sales/age of product

    Potential

    Key contact

- Cop-E-It customer history

  Trade/national account

  Products

  Promotion

  Salesperson

  Key contact

  Potential for up-sell or cross-sell

Internal source data development resources include sales, prospect inquiries, warranty cards, customer service, and promotion activities.

External source data resource analysis identified the following sources of data: company demographic lists, trade shows, sales force lists, industry lists and research, yellow pages (identification of dealers), industry publications, and peripheral product sales. Data on peripheral product sales proved especially valuable. Nothing predicts the use of a copier better than copier paper sales. Of course! Cop-E-It developed a data source in most major markets that had high penetration of bulk copier paper sales. Be creative . . . find a source that, while not directly related to your business, might create an indicator for your business.

Custom source data options for Cop-E-It include business-to-business direct marketing surveys, telemarketing surveys, special promotions, and data share with noncompetitive partners (copier paper marketers).

Cop-E-It did not devote a special program for data testing. Intuitively, they determined that because they lacked almost any data on their business, markets, potential, and customers, anything would help. In addition, Cop-E-It had committed to a data-driven strategy in order to survive against much bigger competitors. The mission of the data development team was to recommend data estimate costs. All reasonable data development efforts would be approved. The company thus moved forward with all areas of data development at the same time.

The source data development strategy created the following data-driven marketing resources for Cop-E-It Corporation:

- Current national account customers ranked by current sales and new or cross-sales potential

- National account prospects ranked by sales potential

- New trade prospects ranked by market and potential

- A relationship marketing program to flag customer problems and new sales opportunities

- A prospect development program for trade ranked by market and potential
- Marketing intelligence:

    Competitive customer identification

    Product/share analysis

    Trade analysis

    Market potential analysis

    Product development insight

    Business planning support tools

Cop-E-It Corporation's external and custom data gathering efforts were quite successful. Because its markets are somewhat limited in target audiences compared to consumer target audience sizes, over 40 percent coverage was developed in year one with a major development effort. Internal capabilities did not produce at an effective level until year two. Internal staffing and other resource requirements caused this effort to lag behind. In year three, Cop-E-It's data-gathering efforts had identified and captured all prospect universes for trade and sales. Data enhancement for propensity to purchase and other marketing activity reached over 50 percent of all records.

All Brands Inc.: Using Source Data Strategy to Reach Competitors' Customers

All Brands Inc. is a national provider of fast-moving consumer products distributed primarily in grocery stores throughout the United States and most of the world. All Brands has many competitors which vary by category of products. All Brands competes in at least ten product categories. Given the many changing marketing dynamics, from increased retailer power to changing consumers to lowered effectiveness of media programs, All Brands has decided to develop a targeted marketing program. Its objectives are as follows:

1. Identify and convert competitors' customers
2. Deliver cost-effective communications
3. Maximize sales to existing customers

To accomplish these objectives, All Brands developed a data proforma "wish list":

- Customer name and address
- Customer demographics
- All Brands products used in customer households
- Promotional sensitivity
- Frequency of All Brands product use
- Users of competitive brands by category
- Demographics on competitive users

A review of internal data development resources suggested that All Brands can develop only limited data as a part of normal business due to limited contact with consumers. Internal data options include coded coupon redemptions, on-pack promotions, and other consumer offers that create a response.

Existing external data options include demographic data, existing survey-driven identification of consumers by category of product purchases, and overlay models of consumer behavior.

Customer data development options for All Brands suggested the following ideas: surveys to identify brand and category users, national multimedia promotions designed to generate consumer names, and joint promotions with key retailers.

All Brands Inc. tested all data development options. Internal data options were limited to coded coupon responses to identify targeted customer households. External data development provided demographic overlays such as age, income, number of children, and so on that can provide means to segment and identify customers by brand propensity. Custom data options, while the most expensive, proved to be a very powerful way to develop a list of users of competitive brands and to identify frequency of use of All Brands customers.

Based upon the proforma analysis, All Brands developed a final data proforma ranked by application and immediacy of impact to the target marketing effort. The data priorities are as follows:

1. Custom surveys to identify customers of both All Brands and competitors by name, brand usage, and categories for multiple brands

2. Coupon coding for identification of customer response and effort effectiveness

3. Demographic overlays for further segmentation of customers/ prospects for targeting programs.

All Brands Inc. is in year four of a five-year plan for data development. They have developed a database of over 30 million households generated primarily by custom or co-op survey efforts. Via demographic and cluster model overlays, they have been able to gain considerable insight into the behavioral and lifestyle characteristics of their customers. They feel that the database has allowed them to communicate directly with almost 60 percent of their primary target audiences by brand and category.

Data-driven marketing applications that are possible due to All Brands' source data strategy include:

1. Targeted promotional programs aimed at users of competitive brands

2. Retention programs for converted households and customer households

3. Identification of customers by frequency of use

4. Grouping of customers by lifestyle attributes such as families with children or healthy lifestyles. This allows All Brands to group products together for better affinity marketing programs.

5. Retail marketing support based upon their database of 30 million customers

6. Targeting of all media based upon insight gained from household-level demographics and models.

While All Brands Inc. feels that the company will always lead with a mass media strategy for brand communications, the database and source data strategy provides a way to uniquely identify and target competitors' customers. In addition, the database will ultimately replace other media for delivery of sales promotion messages.

All Brands Inc. is testing the value of a database to maximize customer relationships across brands and categories over time. As the company learns how to use the power of data-driven marketing and household-level communications more effectively, the database will become increasingly viewed as a strategic resource for the company.

Identifying Source Data Needs by Point of Entry into Database Marketing

Now, you have an understanding of the value of data, the first of the three key building blocks for database marketing. To translate this information to your database marketing requirements, you must conduct your own source data strategy analysis. Once completed, use the matrix in Figure 7-7 to equate your source data strategy analysis to the three points of entry into database marketing.

Figure 7-7   Source Data Decision Matrix

Data Type	Point of Entry		
	Historical Data Management	Marketing Intelligence	Integrated Resource
Customer History	X	X	X
Promotion History	X	X	X
Transaction Data		X	X
Detailed Customer Characteristics		X	X
Customer Data		X	X
Distribution Tracking			X
Related Application Data			X

The matrix illustrates with Xs the types of data usually found in marketing databases associated with each point of entry. This exercise, when combined with similar analysis of your requirements for the other key building blocks of database marketing, will provide insight into your overall entry point and requirements for development of your marketing database.

C H A P T E R 8

Technology: Technology Made Simple

Our number one goal is to break down the barriers between marketing people and the information they need.

Francy Anhut, President, Strategies That Sell

Earlier, we stated that you should not put the technology cart before the marketing horse. That is, you should not get caught up in technology for technology's sake. However it is important that you understand what technology is available. It also is important that technology be harnessed to provide you as a marketer with the information you need to make marketing decisions.

The Importance of Mastering Technology

Cyberphobia is the fear of computers! Most marketers do not break out into a sweat upon first sight of a computer. However, there is a general lack of understanding in the marketing community regarding technical computing and data processing issues. Six years ago, I thought all you had to do was tell the technician to load the names in the computer and you had a marketing database . . . alas, it's not true. In fact, many marketers remain naively unaware of even the basic concepts and approaches required to develop a computer-based application for their marketing programs.

This lack of understanding can at times transform even the most sophisticated marketing executive into a rookie when faced with issues such as system design and structure and data relationships. In fact, the computer software and hardware industry has perpetuated this situation in an attempt to overcome cyberphobia. Statements such as "the database is built in," "no technical knowledge is required," "you can learn the system in two hours," or my favorite, "user friendly," tend to underemphasize the importance of mastering the reasons why a marketing database functions as it does.

While the essence of the concept of database-driven marketing is simple, it cannot be implemented without an understanding of the technical issues involved and the impact of those issues on your database marketing applications.

The challenge to marketers of the 1990s is clear: Reach an understanding with technology. The mission: Master the principles of technology that will drive the success or failure of your marketing database. Technology is one of the three key building blocks of database marketing.

Information from Data

Most companies have a lot of data. Data on almost every aspect of the organization's operations. Many companies even have data on how much data they have. This is especially true for sales and marketing groups as a part of a bigger company.

What are data? Data are facts that represent almost any issue or subject. A data item is the basic unit of a database. Marketing data items could include customer gender, name, address, telephone number, product purchased, promotion code, or any other relevant information or characteristic about your customer (Figure 8-1).

Figure 8-1   What Are Data?

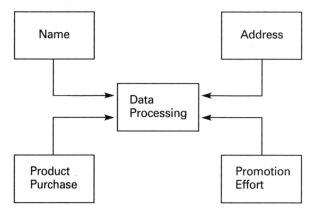

Generally, a company captures basic data that relate to various aspects of their marketing programs. The problem is that individual data items, such as name, product ordered, and so forth have little value other than the facts they represent. It is when items are combined in a manner that facilitates a decision making process that the data has acquired value and become transformed into information.

Data must be transformed into information to be useful. Information, as defined in database marketing, is the organization of data in a manner that will support the decision making process. Data processing systems are the engines that turn the data into information.

The Evolution of Data Processing Systems

In early data processing, the data was processed manually. This was called hand tabulation of data. The first computer systems simulated this manual processing of data. The advantage over hand tabulation was that systems were faster and more accurate. But like manual systems, these early computers tended to focus on one application or task at a time. This approach to data processing is called file processing.

As computer power and sophistication in software applications grew, so did the understanding that data is a corporate resource. Business sought ways to organize and manage their data more effectively. This led to the database form of data processing.

The best way to illustrate the advantages of database processing over file processing is to compare the process and methods.

File Processing Systems

File processing systems computerized the traditional, basic method of processing and accessing data. Such systems are an outgrowth of manual processing. In general, file processing systems, like their manual counterparts, focused on the data processing requirements of *one* set of data items or *one* function of an organization. This is illustrated in Figure 8-2. Customer data is stored in three separate files labeled customer, order, and product. In this example, the marketer is tracking customer data, orders, and product related data separately. The files simply function as a sophisticated rolodex. To access them, or, for example, to get to Jackson instead of Wang on the order file, requires a specific applications program. Each file requires its own applications program. Thus, the applications program written for the customer file will perform the required task on its own file, but cannot access the product file. The application program has no flexibility to process an information request not originally anticipated in the development of that program.

Figure 8-2   File Processing

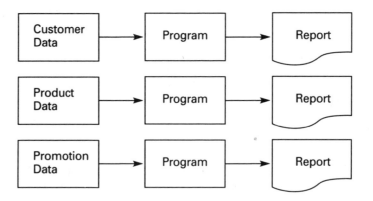

Several limitations to the file processing method of data processing apply specifically to marketing applications. First, as we have seen, file processing is a very inflexible processing method. Each file is its own system and cannot share data with another system and applications program.

Second, file processing systems have a high level of data duplication. Since they require multiple files that relate, but do not interact, similar data is required to track common activity. For example, the customer names Jackson and Wang are stored in the *customer* file to track customer activity. Jackson and Wang must also be stored in the *order* file that tracks order activity. The fact that Jackson and Wang must be stored in two separate files means that there is data duplication. But this cannot be avoided because the customer and order files do not interact.

Database Processing Systems

Database processing systems were developed to overcome some of the limitations of file processing systems. In a database processing system, all data is stored in a single repository called a database rather than in separate files. Figure 8-3 is an example.

Figure 8-3   Database Processing

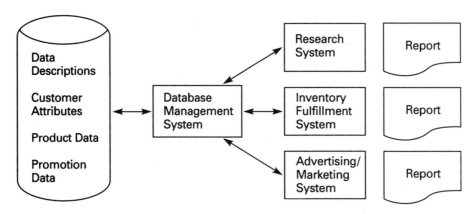

A major difference between the two processing methods is the addition of two important features: a database management system and a data dictionary. These two features are interrelated and form the basis of database processing. The *database management system,* or *DBMS,* is a program or series of programs that create, modify, and control access by applications programs to the information in the database. If multiple data sources are to be compared or combined for decision-making purposes such as comparing customer and promotion data, the DBMS needs only to be instructed on how the data is to be combined in order to perform the process. For example, the data for analysis of promotional programs is generated by the DBMS and the applications programs only format the data into the correct format for analysis purposes. This is called program/data independence. With program/data independence, changes made to the data have less effect on the applications programs.

In file processing, with the file layout built into the applications program, the program would have to be rewritten from two perspectives if we wanted to add a new data element such as age. First, age would have to be added to the "map" of the program that tracks data location. Second, data output formats would have to be restructured to accommodate the new data. In DBMS processing, however, only the applications program would have to change to reflect the additional data in the output.

The database also contains a *data dictionary*. The data dictionary makes program/data independence possible. It contains descriptions of the data in the database. With this information built into the database there is no need for external recording of file formats or layouts as in file processing systems because the structure and content of the database can be determined by simply examining the database. Many DBMSs include processes to easily add new data descriptions into the structure, thus completing the advantage of ease of adding data over a file processing system.

A database processing system overcomes many of the limitations of file processing systems. For example, data integration helps to reduce data duplication because each data element is stored only once in the database. This can reduce computer time to access data in very large systems and increase efficiency. Additionally, when a data item is updated with new information, the updated data is applied to one data item in the database, not to several files as in file processing systems. Because the DBMS accesses the data, applications are not constrained or dependent on file format or layout and have greater flexibility to retrieve, combine, and share data. Thus more information can be created from the same amount of data.

The DBMS is the workhorse of a marketing database. The development of DBMS technology has given marketers the power to combine data in a manner that affects the marketing decision making process.

How Structured Databases Work

Database systems are classified into two loose categories, *structured* or *relational*. Structured databases are further divided into flat, hierarchical, and network forms. Understanding the relationships between data is key in determining which type of structure is correct for your situation. Structured systems have defined data relationships and paths.

The relationship is frequently compared with that between a parent and a child. (This is a weird attempt by a tech person to try to relate to us mere marketing people.)

Figure 8-4

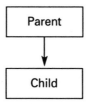

Within a structured database there can be only one of two data relationships. They are one-to-one, with data item A relating only to a single data item B and the pair being accessible only through data item A, or one-to-many, with data item A relating to many data items. Within structured databases, data is organized very simply. There is a natural path or link between data items. The relationship between data items in a structured database are described as parent/child. The parent level of data might be customer name, for example, and the child level of data might be age of the customer. The path is simple because to get to age, you must access the customer by name. The parent/child structure means simple relationship and access to data. Now let's look at the parent/child data relationship in several different structured DBMS approaches.

Flat File Organization

We like to look at a flat file organization as a piece of string.

Figure 8-5

Name/Address   Promotion   Order History

The string contains a series of records or collections of data items about customers or prospects. The string may begin, for example, with a customer's name, address, and phone number. Then it may contain customer characteristics such as age, gender, promotion response, and product or service ordered.

In a flat file, each record can be fixed length, meaning that all records are the same length and can capture only the same maximum amount of information for each data item in the record. In that case, you can only retain a limited amount of data about any given customer. For example, if you only allocate five spaces to sales, you can only track five spaces worth of sales information. Or, the file may have a variable record length. This means that one record can contain more information than the next record and be a different length on the string.

The reason a string is a good analogy for a flat file is related to data access. If, say, you want to access the record on P. Wang, you have to pass Adams, Jackson, and Smith to get to Wang. You cannot go there directly. When you do get to Wang, however, because of the simple parent/child data relationship, all data items that relate to Wang, such as age and gender, will always be in the same place following his name on the string. If you have a fixed-record flat file, the trade-off is that the space allocated may be designed either too large or too small for the data item requirements of your business. If you have a variable file, you may capture so much that the file becomes very large and therefore too expensive to manage and run.

Indexed Flat Files

To overcome some of the problems of the flat file format, many databases are managed in a linked or indexed flat file structure.

Figure 8-6

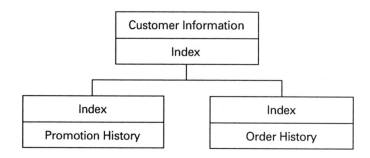

In this case, various types of data are separated out into several strings that are linked together. For example, the parent level in linked files is often called the *customer master* because it contains the basic name and address data on the customer. Other major sources of data items such as promotion history and product order history are stored on other flat file strings. The flat files are linked together by a code that allows the computer to identify them as the same record. This could be a unique identification number such as a social security number, or a computer generated match code made up of pieces of name and address data or some other data. While the parent/child relationship still applies, linked match files allow marketers to access important pieces of information without having to go through all data about a customer or all customers. For example, a marketer might want to identify only customers that responded to the May promotion. In an indexed flat file, the marketer could ignore name and address and first search on promotion, then match by identification code to customer record data. Or if you wanted to select people who ordered product A in certain zip codes, first you would select customer addresses by zip code, then get their identification codes and pull relevant product file records. Many marketing databases are built in some form of linked flat file structure.

Hierarchical Structure

A hierarchal structure looks like a tree. Data is connected by branches. Each entry has only one parent entry and may have several child entries. Data must go from the top of the hierarchical tree and move downward along a predetermined path until it reaches it destination. If a marketer wants to relate data items in different branches of the tree—for example, geography and media code—the computer would have to start at the top of the tree, go down the attribute branch to find geography, return to the top, go down the promotion branch and find the media code, and go back to the top. This seems like a lot of work, but the computer can do it very fast.

Figure 8-7

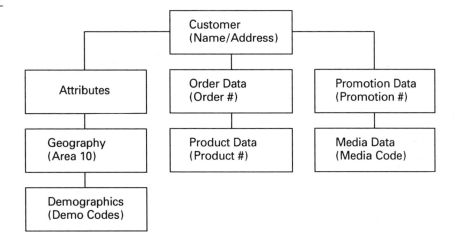

How Relational Databases Work

Relational data organization operates differently than the traditional structured technology described above. The major difference is that in relational databases, there are no predetermined relationships between data items. Data is stored in tables that have rows and columns, and the tables are linked together depending on how the data will be accessed and used for marketing applications.

In a relational database, a table corresponds to a file. A row in the table equals a record and a column in the table equals a data element within the record.

In one table, for example, each row may represent a customer and column data may be attributes such as gender, age, and so on. In another table, the rows may represent promotions and the columns contain customer data. Analysis of the two-table example in Figure 8-8 suggests that the marketer is interested in examining the data relationships of customer to attributes (the table on the left) and promotion to customer (the table on the right). However, the marketer may also want to link customer attributes to promotion data. This is accomplished by having a unique code for each customer that bridges customer Jackson and his attributes in the left-hand table to customer Jackson and his promotion activity in the right-hand table. In a relational marketing database, the tables have many rows and columns and the data relationships between tables are very complex.

Figure 8-8

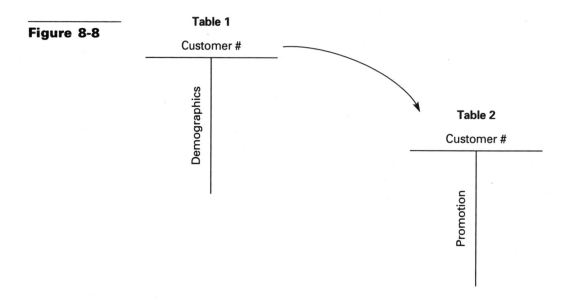

The example below shows how the linkage of data occurs in relational databases. There are several tables including customer, order, geography, promotion, and product.

Figure 8-9

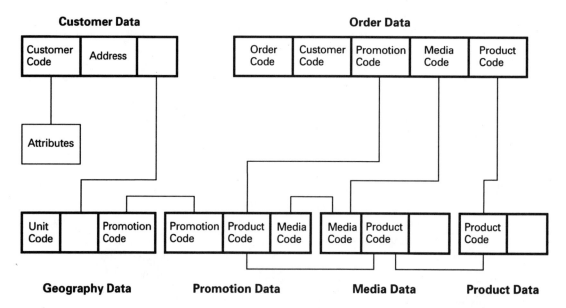

In this example, you can see how the promotion code is linked to geography, order, and promotion information.

It is important in the development of relational databases that the designer understand how the marketer will compare and evaluate the data items in the relationship. Thus, the tables can be set up to facilitate the fastest and most direct access to the desired results. In addition, different relational database software for mainframes and other platforms have unique strengths in implementation of the database and must be chosen accordingly. For example, DB2 by IBM works across a wide array of platforms and hardware. Model 204 by Computer Corporation of America is better at large databases and has a user-friendly access program called Market-Pulse.

Should You Choose a Structured or a Relational Database System?

What database technology makes the most sense for your organization? The answer is that both relational and structured technology may do the job perfectly well. No one particular marketing application can be said to be exclusively suited for a relational or a structured DBMS. Each technology has different capabilities in terms of flexibility and performance—flexibility to examine the detail of the data and the relationship of the customer and your business and performance or the computer power required to accomplish the task.

The following series of questions will serve as a decision screen to help determine which technology best suits your marketing situation:

1. Is your database dynamic?

   Will the data expand or grow over time?

   Will the data be used for multiple applications?

2. What is the size of your application?

3. What are your data access requirements?

4. What is the amount and nature of ad-hoc or unanticipated questions you will want to ask the database?

Compare your answers to the analysis of structured and relational database technology in Table 8-1.

Table 8-1   Comparative Characteristics of Structured and Relational Database Technology

	Structured Databases	Relational Databases
1. Data relationships	Existing, natural simple	Complex, change over time
2. Computer power required	Limited CPU	Greater CPU
3. Points of entry/data access	Limited, parent/child	Almost unlimited
4. Size	Any	Any
5. DBMS development cost	Low/medium	Medium/high
6. Development time	Medium	Low
7. Technical expertise required	Less specialized	More specialized
8. Ongoing management of DBMS	More difficult	Less difficult
9. End user access	More difficult	Less difficult
10. User friendliness	Less friendly	More friendly
11. Ad-hoc query capability	Less capability	More capability
12. Access type	Batch or on-line	Batch or on-line

Advantages of Structured Database Management Systems

As we mentioned, the key decision point in choosing a database management system is the examination of key data relationships and the trade-off between flexibility and performance. Given the restrictions of parent/ child data relationships, data in a structured database needs to form a natural hierarchy or structure. For example, age or order or promotion easily relates back to customer. Structured databases work well if the nature of the data does not change much over time. If you will constantly be adding new data types that are not anticipated in the design process, cost will be incurred on a regular basis to revise the system to accommodate the new data types.

Structured systems offer the ability to more easily access the detailed data linked to a customer name. This may be required in many business-to-business, customer service, or telemarketing oriented applications. Therefore, it is possible to more effectively fine-tune a structured database. If all reports required are consistent and the data is consistent over time, the DBMS can be updated periodically to generate fast, consistent results providing the desired marketing information. Finally, structured files' data relationships need less computer power (CPU) to get the required results. For many marketers this may be an important factor.

To recap, the major indicators for development of a structured database technology solution are as follows:

- Data relationships form a natural hierarchy or order
- Data items do not change much over time
- It is important to access single records
- Detailed fine tuning is important
- Conservation of computer power is important

Advantages of Relational Database Management Systems

Relational database technology offers greater flexibility in examining the "big picture." This is important if your database application has many data relationships and they tend to be very complex. Again, there is a trade-off of performance for this flexibility. Because relational databases are table-driven, the computer must search out the best path to answer the question you have asked. This may require significantly more computer power. For very large databases, the cost for on-line storage and CPU usage can be considerable. However, the resulting feature of ad-hoc capability may more than make up for the limitation. Relational DBMSs allow the user to ask an array of questions that are not predetermined or predefined. This flexibility drives many marketers to a relational database solution.

Relational databases also contain built-in development tools that speed up the development process and allow for prototyping of the system. This means that a relational database can be developed with a small portion of the total records to be included in the system and then loaded with the full file after testing and fine tuning. Relational databases also are more efficient due to less duplication of data.

To recap, the major indicators for development of a relational database technology solution are as follows:

- Flexibility to examine multiple and complex data relationships is needed
- Ability to look at the "big picture" is required
- Storage efficiency is important
- Data access must be flexible
- Development speed is important

At this point, we would like to repeat two points discussed earlier. First, don't choose relational database technology unless it is really appropriate for your marketing application. Beware of third-party database developers that sell only relational solutions. They may steer you to a relational solution because that is all they offer. In our experience, far more databases are built in structured than in relational technology. Second, database development is as much art as science. Two equally talented systems designers, both experts in the same DBMS technology, will choose different paths to get from point A to point Z, your marketing solution. Neither is wrong. This is a highly creative process within basic skill sets of data processing principles.

By this point, we have probably saturated your thirst for understanding of database technology. We hope that you have come away with a basic understanding of the various database structure options available. Now we will turn our attention to a discussion of the hardware platform options for running a DBMS.

Database System Platforms

We will review three primary database platforms available to marketers, mainframes, minicomputers, and personal computers or PCs, plus server technology. The changes in computer capabilities at each of these platform levels has created a dynamic environment for computer hardware. Within the last ten years, most large databases practically had to reside on a mainframe. This was due to computer processing speed, available DBMS software, skilled system designers, and data storage capabilities. Today, minicomputer and PC-based data processing is coming of age. However, there are still practical limitations to both technologies. In the future, there is no question that technology is forcing data access and management down to the lowest possible level. We see this trend today with distributed processing and resulting access to information by multiple users. Dozens of books each year focus on these trends, so we will try to hit only the highlights and the resulting impact on data-driven marketing.

Mainframe Systems

Mainframe platforms still manage the majority of marketing databases. Databases from 100,000 to 100 million records reside on mainframe. The primary advantages of mainframe use are as follows:

- Large storage capacity
- Fast processing
- Multiple applications can be run at the same time
- A large population of skilled developers and technicians to develop and manage systems
- Suited for the background or housekeeping work most databases require
- Compatible with PC and on-line access

Most databases require a great deal of background processing or housekeeping. This activity occurs outside of the database management system. Examples include:

- Merge/purge of multiple files to create net records and householding of databases
- Mailing requirements such as National Change of Address (NCOA), zip + 4, and carrier route coding
- Appending of external data
- Selections and extracts

Most software is still written only at the mainframe level. However, this trend is quickly moving to minicomputers. Additionally, large third-party databases such as NCOA are so large that they must be managed and run on mainframe. Some disadvantages of mainframe use include the cost of the hardware, software, and maintenance staff and facility and the need to share the computer's time with other business functions. Because of the complexity of mainframe software, little "off-the-shelf" software is available that allows access to and analysis of data by nontechnical users. Some mainframe software developers, such as Computer Corporation of America (CPA), have developed user-friendly applications such as CPA's MarketPulse. Fourth-generation computer languages such as Focus also simplify data access. However, even the best applications packages require a level of software language skills to accomplish complex access to data.

Minicomputers

Mini mainframes, or minicomputers, such as AT&T's 3B2 and IBM's AS400, are becoming important in data processing. They can manage most applications in mid-range processing requirements. Minicomputers have a number of advantages. They are less expensive to own, manage, and run. Less technical skill is required to run the system. DBMS software is built into the operating language. Minicomputers are capable of fully functional processing like mainframes. And minicomputers are compatible with PCs or on-line access. Disadvantages of minicomputers include limited processing power and that many software applications are not written for this platform. Many databases housed on minicomputers still require background processing on mainframe. However, we are starting to see some housekeeping programs, such as merge/purge applications, written for minicomputers.

Minicomputers are being used more and more in data-driven marketing applications. One example is the resort and travel industry. Minicomputers run many reservation/hotel management systems and thus are a natural platform for integrated marketing databases. Some suppliers of database technology work in both mainframe and minicomputer platforms. They can process background functions on a mainframe and provide data access on a minicomputer.

Personal Computers

There is certainly no more dynamic category than PCs. For our discussion, we are referring to fixed-location units that serve as workstations, not to laptops or portable computers. However, databases can be accessed with laptops. Three important trends in PCs strike us. The first trend is cost. In the last year alone, computer pricing has brought technology within the reach of every business. There is almost no financial barrier to having personal computers run your business. The second trend is technology. PC processing power, storage capability, and interconnectivity with other computers and systems is growing faster than a nontechnical person can keep up with. The third trend is in software. An array of user-friendly software is available for data access, reports, and analysis. No end is in sight for the growth in sophistication and power of PC software. Use of PCs is growing so fast that there is no question that they are the future of data access and management.

Advantages of PC technology include user-friendly access, less expensive hardware and software, integrated analytical tools, and integrated graphics and presentation tools. However, along with the advantages of PCs come their limitations. PC storage of data is limited. In addition, a PC can only process one function at a time and is usually slower than mainframe or minicomputer processing. Another processing platform must usually be available to accommodate background processing such as merge/purge, file cleaning, and NCOA.

A number of commercially available packaged database programs can manage small databases. These products work well up to the 100,000-record range. While it is possible to manage databases of over 100,000 records on the PC, we have seen very few marketing applications.

Server Technology

Two types of server technology are file server technology and client server technology. File server technology allows multiple PCs to link together in a network of LAN (local area network). The system uses a central storage unit called a server that services all the PCs on the LAN access. File server technology takes advantage of all the benefits of PC access and related programs. However, multiple users have access to the same data set. Multiple requests to a file server can, however, slow down access to data and create situations in which many users can change the core data. This raises data integrity issues. LAN-based processing is all done through the server and not on the PC.

Client server technology extracts a relevant portion of a data set from a database housed on a mainframe or minicomputer and moves it to a PC for processing. Each user in a client server system can have a different level of access or usage. Because the processing occurs on the PC, there are no processing bottlenecks. With the data available on a larger computer, there are also usually no bottlenecks in providing data for download to the PC users. With the trend toward distributed processing of information, with various departments or functions having access to data, client server technology seems to be the preferred method of the future. It offers both the advantages of management of data by a larger computer and the advantages of access and processing at the user level.

An example of client server applications for data-driven marketing would be marketing data shared between product marketing and a research group. The research group might download data for model building, build the model on the PC, and apply it on the database at the higher platform level. Marketing might access some of the same data to generate counts of customers by product purchased or to review responses by program to develop a marketing plan.

Client server applications for data-driven marketing are gaining acceptance rapidly. This approach allows access to information by the groups that need it as well as management of information as a business resource.

The Database Continuum from a Technological Perspective

In Chapter 3, we presented the three key building blocks of database marketing and the continuum of database applications. The decision on which application is right for your business situation is a function of your data needs and where the appropriate database structure and technology platform meets the continuum for your marketing application.

Figure 8-10

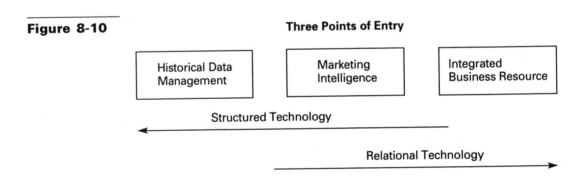

Generally speaking, structured database technology can perform along the continuum from historical data management up to a limited level of integrated business resource application. Relational data technology will start as an option at the low end of marketing information access and continue up the continuum through integrated business resource applications. The overlap in applications generally occurs as a business changes in focus from data capture as the primary function to data access for marketing information purposes.

Technology options vary at the three points of entry along the marketing database continuum. Mainframes, minicomputers, and client server technology can be used at all three entry points. PCs and PC networks can handle historical data management databases, while marketing intelligence and integrated business resource systems require PC on-line access to a higher platform. As a rule of thumb, databases managed at the PC and workstation server level can handle only a limited number of records. We have, however, seen a few databases of over 2 million records with name and address data managed at lower platform levels. Databases at the mainframe and minicomputer level can manage almost an unlimited amount of information based upon processing power and data storage capability.

The information presented in this chapter will help you determine the best data structure, technology, and platform levels for your marketing database program. We have reviewed the three points of entry in terms of where database structure and platforms fall into the continuum. In the next chapter, we will explore the process of building a database for your business.

CHAPTER 9

Technology: Choosing the Right Technology for Your Database

The principles of technology will drive the success or failure of your marketing database.

Database systems have been developed by data processing professionals for many years, for business functions such as human resources and payroll, accounting, and manufacturing-related areas. Development and management of any of the above-mentioned systems required specialized knowledge of both data processing and the application that the database was being designed for. Systems design personnel from inside or outside the company spent many hours working with the future users of the system to understand how to develop the application for their specific needs. Because many businesses use payroll, accounting, and manufacturing databases, a great deal of expertise has been developed over the years.

Balancing Data Processing and Marketing Requirements

Developing a database structure for marketing applications is not very different from the process for other business functions. First, and most important, developing a marketing database requires an understanding of both data processing technology and marketing applications. The two areas of knowledge balance each other in the marketing database development process. Data processing professionals, designing a database management system on their own with no input, would design a very efficient system from the standpoint of access, storage, and efficiency of processing. In doing so, they probably would handicap marketers, who need greater flexibility in using the information in the system for marketing applications. Many times the issue comes down to data processing efficiency versus marketing application performance. This is why both functions must work together for development of a marketing database system that will be acceptable by data processing standards as well as valuable as a marketing resource.

Figure 9-1   Balancing Requirements

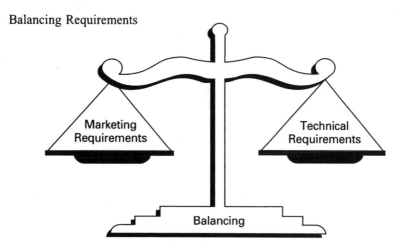

Generally speaking, one of two scenarios exist when a marketing organization starts to develop or significantly upgrade its database capabilities. In one, the business is in synergy on the development of a marketing database application. In this case, data processing and marketing have a close working relationship and have a shared mission to develop a system that will be functional at a reasonable price/performance ratio. In the other, the business is not in synergy on development of a system. Marketing, generally speaking, cannot get resource commitment from data processing and a marketing database is developed outside the purview of an internal data processing group.

More times than not, the second situation is encountered in the business world. Many data processing groups inside a business unit suffer from two major difficulties. The first difficulty is that data processing groups are required to service a wide variety of business functions inside an organization. Usually the primary function, often manufacturing but always the "business of doing the business," has first priority. These data processing groups might like to help marketing, but cannot allocate the resources. In fact, marketing usually has such a low priority that they cannot get even a simple report for information purposes without a delay. In these situations, an antagonistic relationship may exist between data processing and marketing.

The second difficulty is that some data processing groups retain a jealous control over all data processing functions. Such groups may block the use of outside resources by marketing but refuse to commit internal resources. This is usually because the internal group lacks marketing applications experience. The role of the data processing group is limited to providing data to the external system.

Obviously, we hope the scenario that exists in your business situation is one of synergy, wherein all business units, especially data processing and marketing, are working together for a common mission. However, too many times this does not happen. A new buzz-word, *corporate silos,* is an attempt to describe business units or functions within an organization that are entrenched in doing their own functions and lose focus on the combined reason that they exist.

By definition, data-driven marketing applications and thus their databases are intended to be integrated, having the ability to share data and information between related functions. If organizations are not integrated internally, then there is not much chance for the success of data-driven marketing as an integrated resource.

Thus, we encourage all organizations seeking to develop or upgrade their data-driven marketing capabilities to first work toward the following goals: First, bring together the related business functions that would beneficially access a marketing database and create a shared vision of the future of data-driven marketing applications. Break down the corporate silos. Second, create a positive working relationship with the data processing group in your organization. Even if you decide to take your application outside, you will need your internal group. They must provide the data you need to feed your data-driven applications. In many cases, even if they have no marketing applications experience, they can provide valuable input on the data and on interacting with existing computer resources.

Analyzing Your Own Business Situation

Different marketing database system developers have their own analysis techniques, but generally they all come together into a four-step process. The core of the process, no matter how many steps or disciplines are involved, is to involve the user groups into thinking about their organization and their data-driven marketing applications. The four steps ask the following questions: Where are we? Where do we want to be? What does all this tell us? and What do we have to do?

Step 1: Where Are We?

In Step 1, an organization stands back and critically looks at current technology and applications. It assesses the three key building blocks of data-driven marketing and related marketing applications: data, technology, and statistical techniques. Data and research are reviewed in terms of the requirements they place on a database system. The assessment must realistically evaluate current technology and marketing applications. Some questions for review include:

- What are we accomplishing and what can we accomplish?
- How well are we doing it now?
- Can we do better in the future?
- Are there unresolved resource contention issues?
- How good are the working relationships between critical functions?

The answers to these questions are unique to each business situation, as each marketing and technical solution is unique.

Step 2: Where Do We Want to Be?

Step 2 is one of vision for the future. After examining your existing options and restraints, you must move forward to where you want to go with your data-driven marketing application. This process again requires a review of data, technology, and statistical techniques. It starts with an unencumbered vision of the best possible scenario of data-driven marketing within your organization and the resulting technological issues. The process ends in a mutually agreed-upon solution that will accomplish your marketing objectives with sound data processing. This process usually involves some trade-offs. Many items on marketing's data "wish list" will be hard for data processing to provide, and data processing may be reluctant to reach out to embrace applications outside their expertise. The solution may be multiphased, with plans to increase the sophistication of a data-driven marketing system over a series of months or years. Some questions to be asked in Step 2 include:

- What is the extent and nature of data access required?
- What is the nature of the data relationships to be examined?
- What will be the ad-hoc requirements for the system?

- What are the data storage and updating requirements?
- How will the system interact with other systems and functions?
- What is the complexity of the data to be recorded?

Step 3: What Does All This Tell Us?

Step 3 is known as a "gap analysis." This process allows the organization to assess the difference between steps 1 and 2. The process first requires a benchmark of the current usage of database technology and applications, then an assessment of what will be needed to reach your goals. Considerations for this step include financial considerations and restraints, technical considerations and environmental constraints, and data development considerations.

Step 4: What Do We Have to Do?

The purpose of this stage is to form plans to enable the organization to realize its database-related goals. Do not feel that this enablement must be accomplished in one phase or development. Experience shows that development or enablement programs occur along a multiyear timetable. Systems are built in phases based on an organization's ability to adapt to data-driven marketing and to maximize the mix of the three key building blocks. The process results in several plans: A technical development plan; a strategic business plan including source data strategy, applications implementation schedule, and human resource requirements; and a plan for return on investment.

When these four steps have been completed, there is a fifth step . . . implementation! We will explore the implementation process a little later in this chapter.

98 Questions to Ask in Planning Your Database System

Whether you develop your database internally or choose one of many qualified systems developers and managers, you must go through a detailed analysis of your business needs. This process is usually called a *needs analysis* or *system study*. The following is a list of 98 questions for a systems analysis as developed by Donnelley Marketing. While this is not an exhaustive list, it will serve as both a starting point for your analysis process and an indicator of the complexity of the system study process.

Business goals and objectives:

1. What are your business objectives for your marketing database?

2. What key business functions will you require from the database to meet those objectives?

3. Can you prioritize these functions as to their importance?

4. Can you describe your target market/markets?

5. How has your target market changed over the last several years?

6. What changes to you expect to your target market over the next several years?

7. What sources of information do you use to identify your target audience?

8. What are the most important characteristics you would like to know about your customers?

9. Do you have this information currently, how do you use it, and what information do you have from your current systems/files and how do you use it?

10. Are there characteristics about customers that you don't have that might be useful?

11. Do you actively promote to your customer base? If so, please describe, what media?

12. Do you plan to track effectiveness of your efforts, and how will you tie promotions to response data?

Basic customer profile:

13. How many customers do you expect to have in your initial database, from how many sources?

14. How do you distinguish active from inactive customers?

15. Do you have both business and consumer data in your database?

16. Do you identify customers who do not want to receive solicitations?

17. Do you keep prospect data in your database as well as customer data?

18. Do you market to individuals or households or both?

19. Do you want to combine multiple individual records into one household record?

20. Are most efforts ongoing versus single events?

21. Can data collected be pulled together to establish buying patterns?

22. Was the data collected on each file derived over roughly the same period and on an ongoing basis?

23. Can separate fields be successfully merged without losing the identity of the source data from which they were derived?

24. What are the rules and requirements for combining or netting records?

File cleaning requirements:

25. Do you maintain more than one address per customer?

26. Do you want an initial NCOA of the database?

27. Should we use NCOA/NIXIE identification?

28. Should we consider more advanced change-of-address identification besides NCOA?

29. How should addresses be handled that are not correctable by zip + 4 address standards?

30. Will NCOA positive match households be moved, and how will households with no forwarding address be handled?

31. How often will database be change-of-address updated and matched to other suppression/screening files such as a deceased screen?

32. Will the file be processed with DSF (Delivery Sequence File)?

33. Are there specific areas of your data or database that you would like us to standardize or validate?

34. Do you have suppression lists or pander files we need to use?

35. Do you wish us to pass your file against the DMA telephone and direct mail preference files?

36. What should we do with records that are pandered?

37. What else should we know about your customers?

Purchase history information:

38. Do you have purchase history available on customers, both current and historical data?

39. How far back do you want to maintain purchase or other historical data?

40. Are you going to track payment method, and what data should be maintained?

41. Is source of data important to track on the database?

Promotion information:

42. Do you currently track promotion efforts?

43. How do you track responses?

Credit information:

44. Do you keep credit information on customers?

45. How often is this data updated and how?

Demographic information:

46. Do you collect demographic or other customer characteristics?

47. Are you interested in testing demographic overlays?

48. Do you have specific data in mind, or do you need research support?

Reporting requirements:

49. Are there reports you receive on a regular basis now? How frequently and how do you use them?

50. Who uses the reports?

51. How current is the data in the reports, and how current do you want it?

52. Do you have specific requirements for audits or reports following the account, individual, household netting, and database updating process?

53. Are there reports that you need on a regular basis that you cannot get today? How would you like to design them?

54. Do you have samples of existing reports?

55. Are there transaction accounting or auditing requirements that we must provide back to you?

Query/reporting requirements:

56. Describe the type of ad-hoc queries you want to do against the database.

57. What kind of turnaround do you need when requesting counts from your database?

58. How important is it to you to have on-line access?

59. Is interactive on-line access necessary?

60. How many individuals will need to have on-line access to the database at the same time? How many will need to be trained?

61. How many locations will be making inquiries?

62. How much time do you expect to use accessing the database on line?

Selection/extraction requirements:

63. Describe the type of selections performed against the database.

64. What would an average order size be?

65. How frequently will you be requesting mailings or extractions from the database?

66. What outputs do you expect to need?

67. What kind of turnaround time do you need when requesting selections for mailings/telemarketing or modeling?

68. Should we apply pandering files to create/maintain databases for selections from your database also?

69. Will list rental fulfillment be required?

Initial database creation:

70. How many different files or other source data will be input into the initial database creation process?

71. Will existing customer data be used to create the database?

72. Can we get a file format on each file to be included?

73. Will direct mail responses be included?

74. Are any of the data sources in hard copy form and need to be data entered?

75. Are there transaction records to be processed initially either as updates to your current customer file or to create the initial database?

76. What data is contained in the transaction data?

77. Describe any custom reports you want as part of the initial database development process (error checking or frequency distribution, etc.).

78. Will we receive all data sources necessary to compile the initial database?

Database updates/maintenance:

79. How frequently do you expect to update the database?

80. Do you have key dates that we need to schedule updates prior to?

81. Will updates be a complete file replacement or updated data?

82. How many different files will be used in the update process?

83. What historical data needs to be kept in your database?

84. Can we get file formats for each file in the update process?

85. Will direct mail responses be involved?

86. Are any update sources hard copy and require data entry?

87. Are transaction records to be processed for updates?

88. What information will transaction records contain?

89. How far in advance of update date will we receive all files?

90. Will NCOA be done at the update cycle?

91. Will DSF be done at the update cycle?

92. Describe any audit reports required for checking or validation.

93. Describe any custom reports required for the update process.

94. Will overlay data be applied to the update process?

95. Will the same rules for merge/purge and netting apply to update cycles as to initial database creation?

96. When do you expect the first database update to be completed?

Wrap-up:

97. What benefits do you see your company deriving from a marketing database?

98. What challenges must be overcome to successfully implement your database within your company?

The Database Development Process

The process of development of your database will occur in four phases, system design, system development, system implementation, and ongoing system management.

Phase 1: System Design

The system design process is the culmination of the activity we have discussed up to this point. It represents the successful completion of the four-step analysis process discussed previously and a detailed technical needs analysis or system study as illustrated by the 98 questions. This phase's goal is development of a document that covers the following areas:

1. Confirmation of the user's business requirements:

    Programs analysis

    Research functions analysis

    Management implications

    Decision support

    Financial analysis support

    Related functions support such as customer service/distribution/ fulfillment

2. Data requirements:

    Reporting requirements

    Data retrieval

    Environmental requirements

    Security

    Training

3. System characteristics:

    Database/file requirements

    Processing module descriptions/interfaces with other systems

    On-line components, descriptions, and screens

    Reports

    Conversion processing

Specific environment needs:

Hardware

Software

Security

Back-up requirements

Detailed systems flow charts

4. Implementation:

Approach

Development cycle

Staffing

Schedule

5. Cost schedule:

Fixed costs

Development

Equipment

Conversion/load

Training

Ongoing or recurring costs:

Operating charges

Storage

Computer time

Personnel

Reports

Updates

Access to system

Prices of related processing:

Computer printing

Mailing/postal qualification

System upgrades/special programming

Completion of Phase 1 allows you to understand all aspects of the technical development process, and provides management with all the information required to proceed with final approval of system development.

Phase 2: System Development

The system development process represents the physical development of the database structure and the testing of that structure. For relational databases, this usually involves development of a prototype system or small working model. For structured systems, it means development of the code and programs that will store, access, run, and provide reports for the data being managed. This process involves a system designer and several programmers. After the initial development process, data is tested in the system to fine-tune the system and prepare for loading of actual customer data.

Phase 3: System Implementation

The system implementation process is the actual roll-out of your database with live data. All aspects of the system are tested in final form. This includes system access, reports, data quality and completeness, applications support, tracking, and updating. The result is any fine-tuning or program revision that is necessary. As we have stated, database marketing is as much art as science . . . things will not always work perfectly the first time. Fine tuning, testing, and implementation are part of the critical and normal process of database development and implementation.

Many organizations will continue to run an existing system side-by-side with a new one until they are absolutely sure that the new system is functioning as expected. This process can be as short as one month and as long as a year.

Phase 4: Ongoing Management

Phase 4 is the ongoing management of a database system. Generally speaking, both internal and external systems have a manager or administrator, usually called a database administrator or DBA. The DBA is simply the designated contact person for access to and function of the system. Off-line or batch systems are generally stored on tape until some action is required such as a report or update. For these systems, there is very little monthly DBA requirement. On-line or other systems in which organization members interact with data usually require the DBA to monitor and supervise the running and management of the system. This is common practice for both internal and external data management groups.

A Word about Development Timelines and Costs

If your database is custom-developed, your timeline and cost structure will be unique to your applications. If you have a package system, the timeline and cost of your application will be compared to other package applications. For custom systems, there are no absolutes. However, here are some guidelines of typical timelines and price schedules.

Development Timelines

System design/needs assessment:

1. Needs assessment: 1–4 weeks
2. System design document: an additional 2–3 weeks unless the system is very complicated; then the process can take up to 60 days

System development:

1. Initial development: 1–4 months. Six months or longer for complex systems and multiphased systems.
2. Testing: 2–4 weeks

System implementation:

1. No side-by-side operation: 1–8 weeks
2. Side-by-side operation: as much as a year

Ongoing management:

1. Average contract for externally managed system is 1–2 years
2. Internal system life is 3–5 years

Development Costs

System Design and Development

Charges relate to custom development, design, and development. These are typically one-time charges. If a database has a phased implementation over several years or months from one level of technology to another, development charges may be incurred at each phase. Typically, development charges are incurred at the beginning of the process, before the database is up and running. However, many system developers are willing to spread costs over a two- or three-year contract period.

Historical data management design and development charges range from a low of $10,000 to $20,000 to a high of $70,000 to $80,000 for a mainframe-based system.

Marketing intelligence system design and development charges range from a low of $30,000 to $40,000 to a high of $100,000 to $120,000 for a mainframe-based system.

Integrated system design and development charges range from a low of $70,000 to $80,000 to almost any amount at the high end for mainframe-based systems.

PC systems generally have very little associated design. Initial charges are usually less than $20,000 unless you are custom designing a system.

Initial Data Load

Charges for initial data load involve formatting, standardizing, address correction, parcing, postal address updating, merge/purge, householding, NCOA, and any other activity required to develop a clean file ready to load into a database. These charges will generally range from $3 to $10 per thousand for mainframe-based systems.

Ongoing Management of System

Ongoing system management involves access to data via methods from on-line access to batch reports. This activity is quoted based upon the frequency and nature of the marketer's interaction with the database. An off-line database usually has very low ongoing charges for storage of data, and access to the data by report or mailing selections is at a per-thousand rate.

On-line databases will incur charges for disk storage of data, computer time, and other selection charges. If dedicated manpower such as DBA is required, those charges will be incurred on a monthly basis.

Ongoing Updates

Charges for ongoing updates include addition of updated or new information to the database on a periodic basis as requested by the customer. Updates can be on any frequency from daily to quarterly. Charges usually are based per thousand and will be similar to charges for the initial load.

Specific charges for any database application depend on the nature of the system, the degree of access to the database, and the nature of the marketing information required.

Should You Build Your Own Database or Use an Outside Resource?

The decision to develop your system internally versus choosing an outside partner is based upon three considerations: the nature of your application, development requirements, and the importance of the project.

The Nature of Your Application

As we have mentioned, most business information systems groups have extensive experience in development of databases for business functions including finance, manufacturing, and human resources. In fact, many marketing database users have more computer resources than the outside partners upon whom they come to rely. Problems with developing a marketing database usually focus on issues such as priority being given to other business systems and applications, lack of experience in development of marketing applications, an overload on development capabilities, and incompatible systems or other environmental restraints.

Development Requirements

The system may require hardware, software, or scheduling considerations that cannot be met by internal resource groups. The timeline necessary for development and for reacting to changes and user requirements are often major reasons why systems are developed externally. For example, organizations may be limited in database design resources. Database building can require a major use of internal design, programming, and computer time, often overloading other applications and uses. And, many information services groups are not experienced with managing and manipulating the massive amounts of data that can be included in some marketing databases.

Importance of the Project

If the database is not viewed as important to the functioning of the business or as a strategic application, many businesses would rather let someone else handle its development and management. However, if the marketing database application is integrated into other systems, or if other systems will be developed to integrate into the marketing database, the system is often developed and managed internally.

A wide range of external resources are available for development and management of a marketing database system. Some include Axiom,

Donnelley Marketing, Direct Marketing Technologies, Epsilon, May & Speh, Metromail, Ernst and Young, Arthur Anderson, Marc, Neodata, and many others. Generally, suppliers fall into one of two categories. The first is database technology suppliers, whose services are limited to developing and managing database technology. The second is database marketing suppliers, whose services include data, technology, and statistical analysis as well as marketing consulting services.

The major advantages of using an outside resource are listed below:

Fast development and implementation. These companies are experienced in database development, and their timelines will tend to be faster than those of internal development teams.

Expertise. These external providers have developed expertise over a wide array of marketing applications. You can choose a provider that has experience in your area.

Focus. The external provider is building and managing a system only for you. Their focus will be on your application.

Control. If there is internal contention for control and management of the system, this can be eliminated with an outside resource. The marketing group can control all aspects of the use, access, and management of a system provided by an external resource with whom it has contracted.

Of course, there are trade-offs in using an outside resource. The most obvious one is cost. If your system is developed internally, the costs are considered part of operation of the business. Many externally developed programs, controlled by marketing groups, are budgeted by marketing as an alternative use of resources or an increase of expenditures.

As you choose an external provider, you may want to consider whether the system can be transferred to your own computers as an internal resource at a later time. Some system developers will not or cannot allow their database structures to leave their facility. This is a prime difference between a custom system developer and a provider of a packaged system. Custom developers will develop a unique database structure using the appropriate technology for your application which is usually transferable to your computers. Package system providers may not want or be allowed by their license to provide their product to you on an ongoing basis if you choose not to work with them in the future.

The following list of questions may be used in your evaluation of external database development providers.

1. What is the provider's experience in your market and in general?
2. Does the provider have an appropriate industry specialization?
3. How long has the provider been a database marketing vendor?
4. Can on-line access to the database be provided?
5. What functions can be performed on line?
6. What types of database structures are available?
7. Is the technology transferable to your computers?
8. Is housekeeping and merge/purge software available?
9. Is the provider a NCOA/DSF licensee?
10. Are custom or package products to be provided?
11. Will system security be provided?
12. Will the following functions be performed?

    Utilities

    Updating

    Counting

    Householding

    Tracking

    Response analysis

    Modeling/scoring

    Mapping

    PC reporting interface

    Reporting
13. What is the nature of custom applications?
14. Are list selections available?
15. Is list fulfillment available?
16. Are data enhancement overlays available?
17. Does the provider broker lists?
18. Are telemarketing services available?
19. Is site-selection available?
20. Can the system integrate with desk-top analysis systems?
21. Are mailing splits available?

22. Is data entry available?

23. Are creative services available?

24. Is four-color printing available?

25. Are laser printing and personalization available?

26. Is bar coding available?

27. Are lettershop/mailing services available?

28. Does the provider subcontract services?

29. What are the backgrounds of the individuals working with your business?

30. What will be the involvement of senior management with your application?

31. Will full-time access to customer service be available?

32. Is marketing consulting available?

33. What is the turnaround on services?

    Selections

    Merge/purge

    Report development

    Overlay data

34. What is the provider's pricing system?

    Price sheet

    Custom pricing charges

    Package pricing

    Monthly charges for the database relationship

35. What training will be provided for their employees and yours?

36. What is the provider's commitment to your business, industry, and future?

Traditionally, the outside vendor evaluation process starts with a request for information (RFI) from the vendor. This should answer many of the basic questions that will be important to your decision. Next, visit the vendors that have best met your requirements based upon the RFI document. Once you have limited your list to one to three vendors, ask them to bid on the system. This is called a request for proposal (RFP). The marketer must provide the vendors with as much information as possible about the application and requirements. Many times, a vendor meeting is scheduled in which all vendors receive a detailed briefing. This ensures that all are treated equally. Each potential vendor will usually want to conduct a detailed interview before they provide a response. The response to the RFP should include answers to all the questions above and the following:

1. Confirmation of the database marketing application and services required

2. A detailed description of the system design and function

3. A detailed description of the system development and implementation process

4. A description of ongoing management and related processing issues:

   Reports/selections/access/counts

   Updates

5. Support services to be provided:

   Data overlay/enhancement

   Research

   Marketing consulting

   Training

6. A timeline for implementation

7. A cost schedule

8. A contract proposal

9. Back-up and support materials

Point of Entry and Your Database Technology Decision

Technology decisions become more complex as you take into account not only data management structure (software) but platform considerations as well. The decision process involves reviewing both data structure and platform options by point of entry.

The following is an analysis of data structure and platform options for each point of entry: historical data management, marketing intelligence, and integrated business resource.

Historical Data Management

Data Structure

Typically, historical data management systems are managed in an off-line, batch environment. They generate hard-copy reports, mailing tapes, and data sets for further research. They store limited amounts of information, allow limited access to the data, and provide limited flexibility to get at information. Historical data management structures tend to be easy to maintain and to have low cost because they are managed off line and have minimal update charges. These systems are for basic analysis with limited changes to the information over time other than adding new customers, updating responses, and tracking event performance.

Platforms

Historical data management systems can be very large (over 20 million records) or very small (a few thousand records). They will function effectively in a mainframe or minicomputer environment with files of 100,000 records or less. Most mainframe service bureaus tend to require a minimum of around 250,000 records before they will agree to manage a database. Historical data management is suited for small databases on PC or workstation platforms. Many software programs exist for database and lead management programs. Because historical data management systems have no on-line link to a mainframe, PC interfaces with the mainframe tend to be limited to off-line downloads or file samples that are integrated into other PC products for analysis.

Marketing Intelligence

Data Structure

Marketing intelligence databases can be either relational or structured. Many structured databases (flat file or hierarchical) can have sophisticated linking of data. Trade-offs are issues of performance versus flexibility in accessing data. Complex data relationships usually run in relational data structures. Several relational database structures have user-friendly access tools for counting and profiling data.

Marketing information systems include research and decision support tools. More detailed information on customers (such as customer characteristics and transaction data) is present. Relational systems in this category usually provide ad-hoc access. Most marketing information systems have higher costs for data access and management.

Platforms

Marketing intelligence platforms tend to be mainframe-driven. However, many applications have been developed at both the minicomputer and workstation client server levels. PC access also plays an important role. Even if the database is not on line, the PC may be used to download database subsets for reports and analysis. For on-line systems, the PC becomes the primary workhorse of the marketing information access function. This takes the form of counts, modeling and research, profiles, and effort evaluation as well as other management functions.

Integrated Business Resource

Data Structure

Integrated business resources and their marketing applications tend to follow the data processing environment of the overall business system if it exists first. If the marketing database drives the other business application development programs, then marketing functionality can drive the overall system development process. In either case, marketing data and applications are linked to related business functions. These systems have integrated decision making and forecasting tools. Typically, integrated systems can handle any data load required. Most have high costs for data management and access due to the complexity of the system and the data relationships to be accessed.

Platforms

Most integrated systems are mainframe-based. We have observed several driven by linked minicomputer systems. In many cases, the mainframe acts as a server to provide access to relevant information at a workstation or PC level. PC access is used for counting, profiling, reporting, research, and other business planning and intelligence functions.

The decision process that compares platform trade-offs and data structure options at each point of entry is quite complex. Using the information in the above analysis and preceding chapters, you can list the various options for platform and data structure and the positive and negative attributes for each at your chosen point of entry. You may want to conduct this exercise for several variations of platform and data structure. By looking at the process in this manner, you should be able to establish a framework for the technology required for your system.

C H A P T E R **10**

Statistical Techniques: Segmentation—A Key to Understanding Your Customers

It is more important to reach the people who count, than to count the people you reach.

An Enlightened Researcher

Segmentation techniques are presented here as the third and final building block of database marketing. However, they are by no means the least important. Developing your database and filling it with data is only the start of database marketing. Segmentation and other research techniques release the power of the data you have collected.

A Definition of Segmentation

Segmentation comes from the concept that a group can be broken down into smaller parts. The database marketing application of segmentation assumes that all customers or prospects are not alike. The process divides the database into groups or subsets, each with a common set of characteristics and/or behaviors. In the past, as we discussed in the opening chapters, successful marketing meant selling as much as you could to a mass audience. However, this strategy is not as successful today. In fact, we are not sure that, in reality, it ever worked. Nothing can appeal to everyone. Why? Because we all have different needs and wants related to our culture, religion, socioeconomic and demographic characteristics, shopping behavior, and many other factors. Because we are all different, we must identify where, why, and how to sell to consumers and, more important, which consumers we should focus on for our product or service.

The key principles of segmentation are as follows:

- Once a customer has purchased a product or service, he or she is likely to purchase again from the same source, assuming the customer has had a good experience with the original purchase. Therefore, it is important to segment customers from noncustomers. This is the most basic principle of segmentation. Once the database is segmented, the marketer can focus resources on repeat sales to the same customers.

- Understanding the value of customers allows marketers to maximize their business by responding to customers' needs and wants. A business's most valuable customers usually represent a large percentage of its revenue (the 80/20 rule). By learning more about these best customers' needs and wants, the marketer can meet the customers' purchase requirements and at the same time maximize profits.

- All customers do not purchase the same product for the same reason. For example, the two groups purchasing the most aspirin are families with children and seniors. The two groups have different needs and motivations for purchasing the product that would not be met if aspirin were marketed with one universal message.

Segmentation techniques increase marketing effectiveness and efficiency. They make marketing efforts more effective by allowing communications efforts directed or targeted to unique audience segments based upon these groups' needs and wants. Segmentation makes marketing more efficient by allowing marketers to focus resources on target audiences who are likely to maximize the sales effort of the marketer, such as best or most profitable customers.

Using Segmentation in Database Marketing

Outside-In Versus Inside-Out Thinking

The key premise of using segmentation for database marketing is linked to the difference between database marketing and list-driven communications. List-driven communications take an inside-out approach, or "how can I reach my customer?" Database-driven marketing programs take an outside-in communications approach, or "how can my customer reach me?" Database-driven marketing creates the opportunity for a dialog or relationship with the customer. This concept has created a fundamental change in marketing research thinking. Research is no longer a project, it is a process. It is an ongoing relationship with the customer. The process may involve customer service, returns, exchanges, referrals, additional purchases, and many other interactions. Outside-in thinking allows us to view customer behavior as the driver determining our next marketing tactic. We ask questions such as what do our customers want? What are they telling us? Why are they not buying? Why are they returning products or calling customer service? Customers start to influence our thinking process. This process creates information sharing. The customer is no longer only marketing's customer, he or she is the company's customer. The customer's entire process of contact with the company is examined.

Discovering Mutual Interests of Customers and Marketers

The database allows us to pay attention to the mutual interests of our customers and ourselves as marketers. A couple goes to their favorite restaurant every Friday night. One particular Friday evening they enter and only a table for four is open. The manager decides to ask them to wait for 20 minutes for a table. His reasoning is that he will generate more revenue from four people than from two if a group of four walks in the door. The couple is upset and leaves without eating. The manager has forgotten to look at the value over time of the customers who walked away. For example, at $35 per visit times 20 or 30 visits per year for 10 years, the value of these customers comes to $7,000 to $10,000 lost in the gamble that one four-top table might turn an additional $35 on that Friday night. An alternative scenario might be as follows: the manager, recognizing the couple as regular customers, not only gives them the four-top table but thanks them for being regular customers and offers them a free appetizer for their patronage.

A database allows us to manage the prior knowledge we gain on a customer and determine the customer's expectation. Consider the scenario of the couple in the restaurant. What if they walked in, were seated, and were automatically served a bottle of their favorite wine, or were asked, "Would you like the usual?" This is a very powerful use of information as a shared benefit. The principle is the same for customers at a restaurant or at a bank with 40 branches and hundreds of thousands of customers.

Keeping Up with the Data

Analyzing a mailing list can be compared to taking a quick photograph of a tree—point and shoot. In contrast, research in a database is more akin to photographing a fast-running gazelle. The problem for the researcher is, How do I catch up? Is it possible that my customers are changing faster than my research time-lag? In the past, 19 to 20 months was considered a good average time for designing and bringing a new product to market. Today, marketers have to do it in a fifth of the time due to competitive pressures. It is hard for research to keep up with the pace. If you have a list of customers you want to survey, first you select a sample. Then you design a survey, mail it, and allow time for return of the survey and tabulation and analysis of the results. Two to three months' work just to gather information. A database, however, is a vehicle with constant inflow of customer data. It allows for generation of intelligence much faster than the research processes of the past. As stated previously, database research is a continuing *process,* not a one-time project.

The most important factor to researchers for database segmentation is data. If the database is stocked with the wrong information or inaccurate information, the results will be disappointing. Garbage in . . . garbage out. Nine important attributes of data that affect database segmentation are time gap, accessibility, integrity, perishability, freshness, ongoing updates, accuracy, quality, and cost.

Time gap reflects the timeframe in which the data was received compared to the point in time at which the research was conducted. For example, you may do a quarterly analysis of sales, but sales come in over a period of three months. Data must be available for the period of time and in natural sequence compared to the research project. To be *accessible,* the data must be organized by the right pattern for the analysis you want to conduct. Otherwise, you may have a hard time accessing the information you require.

To have *integrity,* information must be managed in a way that ensures that like data is stored in the same manner and that unanticipated data that affects research results is captured. *Perishability* refers to the shelf-life of the data. How often will the information change? Data does not last forever because people change. *Freshness* refers to how recent the data is. Basing results on old data that has a chance of perishing will lead to disappointing results.

If *ongoing updates* are not undertaken, results may not be accurate as your customers change over time. The *accuracy* of your data should be examined. Does it have biases? For example, how many records have phone numbers or data on children in the household? Does the data have consistent *quality* throughout the data set? Is the information consistent record to record and does it cover enough records to accomplish your objectives? Most external and internally developed data is acquired at a *cost*. This cost must be analyzed to justify the purchase in terms of the customer-related payout.

Segmentation and Your Database

Your House File

The core of your marketing data is a house file. The house file represents the transaction and customer data that is proprietary to your business. Segmentation can prioritize this information and make it more relevant to you. For example, if you sell lawnmowers, knowing that your potential customer has a back yard with grass will help. The house file is your opportunity to collect relevant data into your database. Some marketers say, "I have 35 million records in my database . . . how many do you have?" The size of your database is not the key. The important thing is the relevance of the data. For example, two variables predict whether a person will buy a word processor software program—computer access and ability to type. A segmentation strategy can help organize data to prioritize the key variables that will make a difference for your marketing applications.

Choosing the Right Analyst

A researcher charged with implementing segmentation programs for database marketing applications must have skills in statistical techniques and modeling (see Chapter 10), an understanding of computer language, and knowledge of query language. However, the most important skill is customer insight or knowledge of the marketing application. The worst thing you can have is a super statistician who knows nothing about your customers. The output will not be actionable. Make sure that you hire a researcher who can communicate with marketers.

A skilled database researcher can organize, reduce, summarize, analyze, and manipulate information; identify relationships; predict behavior; and develop controls, among other skills. This translates into characteristics associated with successful segmentation:

- Segmentation should provide the capability to distinguish between characteristics of good customers and marginal customers.
- The characteristics chosen for segmentation should be actionable and available.

- The characteristics chosen for segmentation must be measurable.
- The process of segmentation must be cost-effective.

Types of Segmentation

Types of segmentation include:

- **Demographic segmentation.** Demographics are information that relate to an individual, household, or group of individuals or households. They are the core of database segmentation. Demographics describe the physical characteristics of an individual and are stable over a period of time. Examples include age, income, family size, home ownership, occupation, sex, and marital status. Typical database segmentation projects would include ranking and sorting customers and prospects by demographics or ranking and sorting products and services by demographics.

- **Behavioral or psychographic segmentation.** Psychographics attempt to describe people's behavior: what they spend money on, what they do in their leisure time, their lifestyles, and so on. Information is collected via surveys or built into cluster-driven software products such as Prizm or MicroVision.

- **Geographic segmentation.** This type of segmentation compares where consumers live. For example, a marketer may examine differences in customers and prospects by region, ZIP code, state, or census tract, or even compare one group of households to another.

- **Offer segmentation.** This type of segmentation compares customers or prospects who have received offers or promotions that are being tested or used by the marketer.

- **Benefit segmentation.** As we mentioned above, different target audiences purchase the same product for different reasons. Benefit segmentation attempts to correlate specific product benefits with the target audience motivated to purchase by such benefits.

- **Product segmentation.** Product segmentation correlates the characteristics and needs or wants of the target audiences using the product. With product segmentation you identify which target audiences purchase the product and thus represent the greatest revenue potential for the product, as well as the purchase dynamics of these segments.

- **Product usage segmentation.** This segmentation relates usage to target audience segments. It helps identify product potential and strength or weakness in marketing efforts. A benefit of product use segmentation is identification of niche marketing opportunities. Segmentation will identify current audience niches as well as target audience segments that are not purchasing the product or service. Marketers can then conduct benefit and product segmentation to repackage or communicate differently to identified niches.

- **Purchase segmentation.** This segmentation technique identifies the relationship between the consumer's purchase of your product and your company. For example, a consumer may be a frequent and loyal purchaser or be trying the product for the first time, or may be buying only by promotion. Generally, consumers can be classified into the following purchasing segments:

  1. Frequent or loyal users

  2. Competitive, loyal, or frequent purchasers

  3. Switchers, who have no loyalty to a brand

  4. Promotion buyers, who purchase on price or other promotional incentive

  5. Not in category—consumers who do not or have not purchased in a category

Each of the five segments can be broken down into subsegments based upon unique purchase needs or wants.

Getting Actionable Results

The analyst converts large amounts of data into information. Database analysis is not an isolated entity—it relates to all data-gathering and management functions. If other management areas are not performing well, data analysis will not perform magic. Data is like your dirty laundry—without organizing and sorting it, you cannot process it well. For the analyst and the process of database analysis to function effectively, the proper environment must be established. Responsive action requires a culture inside your organization. The business needs to feel comfortable reacting to information. We ignore a lot of information because we don't see its consequences. Thus, a system needs to be in place to encourage the use of information and to reward those willing to take risk to create change. Make sure that the analysis and action that is created by your research process causes learning. Too many times, an organization does not learn from the research process.

Segmentation and Reaching Your Customers

Finding Your Best Customers

Customers are not alike. You must organize your customers from your best to your worst. It is more than likely that the 80-20 rule will apply: 20 percent of your customers will account for 80 percent of your business. This is the first basic pattern that you will observe in your database.

The only reason you are conducting research is to gain competitive advantage. In a military maneuver, you would never move your troops to a location only to realize that your enemy has more fighters and arms. Your competitive strategy must be communicated to your researchers in order for them to focus on the important outcomes of analysis. A database researcher can help develop methods that will support your competitive advantage by taking advantage of market conditions and developing new customers.

The following is a list of strategic database research outcomes that can be implemented in your business situation:

- Increase loyalty
- Generate repeat business
- Cross-sell
- Create niches
- Identify prospects
- Reduce costs
- Market smarter
- Form better distribution channel relationships
- Increase promotion effectiveness
- Identify customer value
- Improve lead qualification
- Increase traffic
- Lower customer drop-out
- Increase customer satisfaction

Creating a Dialog with Your Customers

Another function of analysis is to stimulate the process of customer interaction. This process uses imaginative marketing techniques that offer customers a variety of methods of communication with you. By creating a two-way communication or dialog with customers, marketers generate valuable information that will affect future exchanges with the customer and feedback on the customer's relationship with your company. This process generates continuous improvement to the database marketing program. Most marketers enjoy gaining new customer relationships, but few enjoy maintaining those relationships. It is important that the process of interaction does not create customer expectations higher than you are willing to meet over time.

Your Database as a Channel of Information

We are familiar with channels of distribution—places to sell products, and with channels of communication—magazines, television, radio, and so on. Databases create a new channel . . . a channel of information. The database as a channel of information brings together all communications and distribution information into a complex customer-based roadmap. If developed properly, the database as a channel of information can be a powerful resource. By analyzing historical data, purchase behavior, and use of segmentation and modeling techniques, marketers can master the information distribution process to manage all customer contact.

Interacting with Your Customers

By definition, your database is an interactive resource. If your marketing efforts make promises to customers, make sure that you can fulfill them. An analytical program can conduct probability analysis to monitor promise fulfillment, consistent treatment, and customer relationships throughout the customer buying cycle. This is accomplished by establishing multiple contact points with the customer over time and monitoring repeat purchases. You can then develop a value for that customer over time called a lifetime value calculation.

Some proactive interaction techniques include:

- Suggestive selling
- Value-added offers
- Relevance
- Timely communications and offers

- Uncertainty absorption (individuals have a limited capacity to handle new information, things, and circumstances)
- Procedural justice—if you have a customer problem, make sure that the resolution process is perceived as fair, friendly, and unbiased by the customer

Managing Your Customer Relationships

Customers are our key asset and a marketing database provides a way to manage our customers better. We accomplish this through descriptive techniques generated from the historical data we capture about customers. This process creates intelligence out of data. Symptoms of poor or inadequate customer management include:

1. Inconsistent communications
2. Inaccurate timing of messages
3. Impersonal treatment
4. Intrusive communications
5. Too many communications

Generally, these conditions occur because systems are inadequate to provide correct information, not enough information is available, management does not properly direct customer management issues, or no measurements for success are in place for managing customer communications.

A marketing database and segmentation analysis can help marketers develop a customer management program. Generally, customer management programs have three major objectives:

1. **Acquire appropriate customers.** Switch from a strategy of trying to acquire any customer to acquiring profitable customers.
2. **Retain best customers.** Focus on keeping all the customers you acquire.
3. **Reactivate desired former customers.** Seek out and reactivate former customers.

You can accomplish this by establishing a customer intelligence resource out of your database. This requires that you capture the right customer data and develop analytical techniques that prioritize your customer information. The output of this resource will be ongoing communications and sales to your customers. Segmentation techniques will help you select target segments, establish measurable segment goals, and evaluate the effectiveness and efficiency of your ongoing customer management program. Tasks for analysis include:

- Ensure customer satisfaction
- Analyze customer feedback
- Establish customer expectations
- Encourage customer referrals
- Develop a customer network
- Create future customer relationships
- Orchestrate total marketing communications to customers
- Maximize the long-term customer profit stream

The key challenges you face as you develop a customer management program is to first put yourself in your customers' shoes. Encourage all managers to treat customers as they would want to be treated. Second, attempt to stay a step ahead of your customers. Anticipate their needs and wants.

26 Customer Analysis Programs to Consider

The following 26 customer analysis programs are worth considering for your applications:

1. **Customer count analysis.** A gains and losses analysis
2. **Customer gains analysis.** Why and how did we gain new customers?
3. **Customer losses analysis.** Why and how did we lose our customers?
4. **Customer migration analysis.** How customers are migrating among products and how they can be resegmented
5. **Customer profile analysis.** Analyzing your customer segments
6. **Customer segmentation analysis.** Segmentation of customers by the characteristics mentioned previously in this chapter
7. **Customer solicitation analysis.** Effectiveness of communications programs
8. **Customer response analysis.** Documentation of our acquisition investment in our customers

9. **Customer promotion analysis.** Evaluation of communications programs

10. **Customer purchase pattern analysis.** Evaluation of patterns of purchases over time by customer subsegments

11. **Customer price sensitivity analysis.** Evaluation of price, price changes, discounting, and other price-related issues and customer purchases over time and for a specific point in time

12. **Customer seasonality analysis.** Differences in purchase patterns through the calendar year

13. **Customer purchase occasion analysis.** Reasons for customer purchase such as life-stage event

14. **Customer payment method analysis.** How soon and by what method did customers pay?

15. **Customer spending analysis.** Analysis of customer spending by segment and individual for a point in time and over a period of time

16. **Customer channel analysis.** Analysis of the channel or channels through which the customer purchases (for example, catalog and retail)

17. **Customer purchase location analysis.** Analysis of the location of customer purchase activity and changes over time

18. **Customer network analysis.** The decision support system and its effect on the purchase process

19. **Customer needs analysis.** Customers' requirements for purchase of product including information requirements

20. **Customer wants analysis.** How the customer wants to be sold

21. **Customer priority analysis.** The purchase priority of products and services (for example, clothes and food may be purchased before luxury items or gifts for the grandchildren)

22. **Customer change analysis.** How customers or customer segments are changing over time: lifestyle changes, demographic changes, geographic changes, and customer perception changes

23. **Customer benefit analysis.** Organization or prioritization of benefits for customer segments

24. **Customer motivation analysis.** Required motivation for purchases, migration, and so on.

25. **Customer social concern analysis.** Is it important to react to customer concerns such as the environment or privacy?

26. **Customer investment analysis.** Customer profitability at a point in time and over time, including lifetime value analysis and future profit-stream analysis by customer and by customer segment

Your ability to conduct the above analyses will depend on your ability to access two types of customer data in your marketing database. The first type is behavioral data. You must capture the correct transaction-related data to apply the segmentation analysis. Second, in order to implement some of the customer programs listed above, you must have access to some inferential information gathered via survey or sampling and applied over the larger database.

How to Develop Your Customer Management and Segmentation Programs

The "Continual Improvement" Approach

Gysan is a Japanese word and philosophy which means "continual improvement." We must apply this approach to customer management in database marketing. To develop a list of preferred customers we must have the customers' prior history to conduct analyses. We must also create frequent interaction with them and develop a special relationship based upon a different status, extra services, or personalized incentives. This must be a relationship mutually beneficial to the business and the customer . . . think of it as a relationship contract.

The four basic premises behind customer management are:

1. You must commit to tracking, managing, and appreciating the lifetime value of your best customers

2. Do not underestimate the intelligence of your preferred customers

3. Empower your best customers—let them participate in your marketing process

4. Empower your employees

We hope the analytical techniques and processes we have described will inspire you to view your marketing database as a customer management resource. When viewed in this manner, a database is not an expense or even an investment, but a revenue producer and a profit-maximization tool.

Six Steps to Segmentation Program Development

Developing a process for implementing segmentation analysis has six steps: organizing data, defining data, managing the right data, accessing the data, processing the project, and analyzing the results.

Organizing the Data

Organize your data by conducting the source data strategy recommended in Chapter 7. Develop a data proforma and test and gather all the relevant data to conduct the segmentation projects you intend to implement.

Defining the Data

Define the data elements to be used and their location, as well as other relevant information relating to each data element such as when collected, how collected, and when updated.

Managing the Right Data

As explained earlier, you must develop an appropriate database management structure to capture and manage the data required for segmentation. You must be able to:

- Capture and manage historical data
- Add other data such as enhancement data as appropriate
- Extract data for analysis
- Attach appropriate scores or other segmentation output to the master file
- Be able to select from the database by the scores
- Gather, manage, track, and report feedback to programs

Accessing the Data

You must build in appropriate access to the relevant data for analytical programs. This may be on-line access, extracts for analysis, or analysis tools built into the database processing functions.

Processing the Project

Your system must be set up to effectively and efficiently process the relevant data to develop the segmentation project. This may sometimes take several steps and involve several computer runs. If this activity is done on a mainframe, it can take significant time and cost. Often, jobs will abort and must be rescheduled on the mainframe, causing delay. Most research projects today are implemented at the PC or workstation level to eliminate delays and take advantage of user-friendly programs with graphics and word processing functions.

Analyzing the Results

This is the most important part of the process. Make sure the analyst who is interpreting the results of the segmentation project understands the marketing objectives and database marketing applications. Much of interpretation of results depends on understanding how the results apply to a certain situation. This is based on experience.

Of the three key building blocks of database marketing, segmentation is often least appreciated. Most marketers are willing to make a commitment to the first two building blocks, technology and data capture. However, that same commitment is commonly lacking when it comes to providing ongoing resources for necessary segmentation and research. Technology and data standing alone, without segmentation tools, have only limited value. This is the heart of the Great Database Marketing Paradox. Database marketers must commit to research and segmentation tools as only they provide the power to unlock the data and technology to which they have already committed.

Statistical Techniques: Analysis and Modeling

Determining where you want to go, then working backwards to figure out how to get there, is likely to yield . . . valuable data leading to fruitful decisions.

Alan R. Andreasen, "Backward Marketing Research,"
Harvard Business Review, May/June 1985

The ability to predict future customer behavior can give you the marketer a significant competitive advantage and increase level of control over your marketing investments. That's the reason for learning how to use and using the statistical techniques illustrated in this chapter. It is important to remember that the purpose of analysis and modeling is not to build the world's most sophisticated statistical model. Rather, the primary objective is to gain customer insight, improve marketing efficiency, tailor products and services to the right customer segments, achieve higher profitability, and develop long-term customer relationships.

The right historical data and statistical tools can enable you to predict how a prospect or customer will behave both in the near future and over the long term with a reasonable degree of accuracy. This chapter seeks to explain the power of predictive models and show how end results of modeling can often be relatively easy to understand and use. The main focus is to help you employ the results of statistical analysis and modeling to better understand customers and manage profitability. In other words, rather than describe statistics, statistical formulas, and methodologies for their own sake, we will examine the marketing, financial, and managerial implications of database-driven research and analysis.

Begin with the End in Mind

An effective approach to managing research projects is to begin with the end in mind. This has been described as *backward marketing research* by Alan R. Andreasen.[1] His premise is that the best way to design usable research is to start where the process usually ends and then work backward. In other words, how will the information that is gathered be used? What should it enable the marketer to do? A marketer working with a researcher first defines the required *end result* of a research project *before* determining what their first steps in conducting the research will be. This backward planning allows the researcher to better understand how the modeling output will be actionable to the marketer.

All too often, research reports gather dust on managers' shelves because the information they contain, while it may be of some interest, is *not* actionable. In order to ensure usable research, a marketer needs to understand exactly what research can deliver, and the researcher must understand how the research will be used.

Before any research project is undertaken, both the marketer and the researcher should have a good understanding—and the *same* understanding—of how the results will be used. The managerial considerations can include the planned uses of the scoring model (we recommend the use of a scoring model in conjunction with the use of all statistical techniques), clearly examined and described, and projections of how current marketing and promotional practices will be improved through the use of the scoring model. The marketer and researcher can then begin to choose the appropriate data-gathering method and statistical analysis required to conduct the research.

Using Scoring Models to Predict Customer Behavior

In general, scoring models are designed to predict how individuals will behave in the future. A score is assigned to each individual in the customer database according to the individual's propensity (or likelihood) to respond or purchase. High scores are assigned to the individuals predicted to be desirable to the company, and low scores are assigned to individuals projected to be less desirable. This process enables a marketer to rank every customer in the database, from those having the greatest profit potential to those that have the least. This ranking will influence a marketer's decisions about how to treat different customer segments according to their potential profitability. We will begin by describing a typical report resulting from a scoring model, called a *gains table,* shown in Table 11.1.

Table 11-1   Profitability Gains Table

Decile	Number of Customers	Percentage of Customers	Cumulative Number of Customers	Cumulative Percentage of Customers	Average Predicted Future Profit per Customer	Total Predicted Future Profit per Cell	Cumulative Predicted Total Future Profit	Cumulative Average Predicted Future Profit per Customer	Cumulative Percent of Maximum Profit
1	24,000	10%	24,000	10%	$19	$456,000	$456,000	$19	34.55%
2	24,000	10%	48,000	20%	$15	$360,000	$816,000	$17	61.82%
3	24,000	10%	72,000	30%	$11	$264,000	$1,080,000	$15	81.82%
4	24,000	10%	96,000	40%	$7	$168,000	$1,248,000	$13	94.55%
5	24,000	10%	120,000	50%	$3	$72,000	$1,320,000	$11	100.00%
6	24,000	10%	144,000	60%	($1)	($24,000)	$1,296,000	$9	98.18%
7	24,000	10%	168,000	70%	($5)	($120,000)	$1,176,000	$7	89.09%
8	24,000	10%	192,000	80%	($9)	($216,000)	$960,000	$5	72.73%
9	24,000	10%	216,000	90%	($13)	($312,000)	$648,000	$3	49.09%
10	24,000	10%	240,000	100%	($17)	($408,000)	$240,000	$1	18.18%
Total	240,000	100%	240,000	100%		$240,000			

Using a Gains Table to Project Customer Profitability

A gains table gives the marketer an indication of what can be gained from the scoring model. Using the results contained on a single page, you can project and manage the profitability of each customer segment.

Because the scoring model is often designed to differentiate profitable from less profitable customer segments, you can use this information to maximize the return on marketing investment by guiding the allocation of marketing resources.

The scenario reflected in the gains table (Table 11-1) is an example. The customer base shown, comprised of 240,000 individuals, can be divided into ten equally-sized segments, or deciles, each of which represents 10 percent of the total customer base. The gains table ranks these deciles, each with 24,000 customers, by the predicted future profit potential of each customer segment. Decile 1 represents customers with the highest profit potential, and Decile 10 represents the segment with the least profit potential.

The gains table identifies the segments that are profitable to the company (Deciles 1, 2, 3, 4, and 5) as well as segments that are not profitable (Deciles 6, 7, 8, 9, and 10). The gains table immediately draws attention to the best segment, Decile 1. This decile is estimated to bring in $456,000 toward future profit (an average of $19 per customer). The second decile, with an average projected profit per customer of $15, predicts a total future profit of $360,000. Cumulatively, these top two deciles represent $816,000 in predicted total future profit and a $17 cumulative average predicted profit per customer (cumulative profit divided by the cumulative number of customers).

The predicted profitability of the deciles decreases following the ranking process. The gains table shows that Deciles 1 through 5, representing a total of 120,000 customers or 50 percent of the entire base, result in a positive profit flow. In fact, the maximum profit for the company is estimated at $1,320,000. Decile 1 accounts for only 10 percent of the customer base but represents 34.55 percent of the maximum predicted profit. Deciles 1 and 2, with 20 percent of the customers, account for 61.82 percent of the maximum profit. The top 30 percent of the customer base, Deciles 1, 2, and 3, represent over 80 percent of the company's maximum potential profit. Deciles 6 through 10, on the other hand, are not profitable to the company and result in a negative profit flow. The sum of all deciles is $240,000 in predicted future profit.

The gains table can have significant implications for both new and experienced database marketers. The table can be used to identify the optimum strategies for allocating marketing resources: which customer groups to target and which to avoid. In addition, the marketer can also conduct an ad-hoc analysis to profile the characteristics of the customers in each decile. Using this information, marketing communications can be customized to fit specific needs, wants, and requirements. As a result, marketing efforts can focus on the deciles that will maximize company profitability, which in this case may represent half of the entire customer base.

The gains table analysis usually reinforces the basic customer management principle that all customers are not created alike. It also allows a marketer to examine whether conventional marketing wisdom, such as the concept that a small proportion of customers produce a large percentage of the profits, is applicable to the company's customer base.

However, the value of this kind of gains table and predictive modeling is largely based upon a marketer's ability to predict future customer activity. The next question is how a marketer can go about predicting an individual's future behavior.

Ask the Right Questions

In one popular childhood game, "Twenty Questions," one person thinks of an object and another has up to twenty chances to ask questions about its size, color, shape, and so on. The goal is to guess the imagined object using as few questions as possible. Winning the game is determined by a player's ability to think of the most revealing questions to ask. Predicting customers' future profit potential works in the same way.

A scoring model is developed by analyzing and predicting customer behavior tendencies. A marketer collects various data about customers and prospects, seeking to predict how they will behave in the future. However, first the marketer needs to use marketing imagination to create a list of good questions.

To a certain degree, customer behavior is predictable. If you can understand customers' needs and wants, their lifestyle and life stage, their past buying habits and purchase timing, then you are more likely to ask the right twenty questions and better predict a customer's future behavior propensity.

Let us consider the example of a book retailer who is thinking about focusing marketing and promotion dollars to effectively target an appropriate customer segment. The retailer is considering asking customers the following questions in order to predict their future buying propensity for a cookbook series.

Demographics:

What is their gender?

Male
Female

What is their age?

Young adults
Middle age
Older people

What is their education?

High school
College
Graduate school

What is their occupation?

White-collar worker
Blue-collar worker

What is their marital status?

Single
Married

What is their residential environment?

Urban
Suburban
Rural

Purchase history:

What books do they purchase?
Fiction or nonfiction
Hard cover or paperback
Best seller or "critically acclaimed"

When was the last book purchase made?
Last week
Last month
Last year

How frequently do they purchase books?
Once a month
Every three months
Every six months

How much do they spend each year on books?
Ten dollars
Fifty dollars
One hundred dollars

Psychographics:

What is their level of deal proneness?
Always buy on sale
Sometimes buy on sale
Never buy on sale

Lifestyle:

What are their interests?
Gourmet cooking
Wines
Dieting/weight control
Fine art/antiques
Foreign travel
Health/natural foods
Avid book reading
Buy prerecorded videos
Casino gambling

After identifying these possible questions, the bookseller needs to identify which question, or series of questions, will be most relevant to predict future buying behavior.

Learn from Experience

There are two basic ways that this retailer can select the right predictive variables—in other words, ask the right questions. The first approach is to examine existing customer data and conduct a statistical analysis to determine the relationship between historical profitability and various demographic, psychographic, lifestyle, and purchase characteristics. Profiling the dominant characteristics of the retailer's current best cookbook buyers often is a very useful step in learning to predict future customer behavior. Alternatively, if customer data is not available, the marketer can conduct a customer survey or design a test promotion. The relationship between self-reported future purchase intention and various customer characteristics can then be ascertained from the survey results.

Both of these approaches will give the retailer an understanding of the right questions to ask in order to identify profitable future cookbook-buying customers. In this example, based on multiple linear regression analysis (see page 182), the retailer discovered that the following sets of characteristics were most helpful in projecting the future profitability of cookbook customers: gender, amount spent on books each year, and certain lifestyle interests.

The retailer learned that females who spent more than one hundred dollars on books and were interested in gourmet cooking and wine were the customers most likely to purchase cookbooks. Knowing the answers to these four relevant questions helped the retailer gain insight about whether or not a customer or prospect would profitably respond to a planned cookbook series.

In addition, the retailer needs to know whether these four questions varied in their relative importance in terms of predicting potential customer profitability. Based on multiple linear regression analysis, the retailer again found out that the most important predictor was spending one hundred dollars on books. A value of 10 points was assigned to that variable. The second most important predictor was the gender of the customer, with a value of 8 points attributed to females. Finally, interests in gourmet cooking and wine were assigned point values of 5 and 6, respectively.

Demographics:

What is their gender?

Male	0 points
Female	8 points

Purchase history:

How much do they spend each year on books?

Ten dollars	1 point
Fifty dollars	5 points
One hundred dollars	10 points

Lifestyle:

What are their interests?

Gourmet cooking

Yes	5 points
No	0 points

Wine

Yes	6 points
No	0 points

The retailer has now created a scoring system and can assign each customer a score indicating the propensity to purchase cookbooks. The retailer can use this scoring system to rank the potential of the 240,000 customers from high to low.

For example, Customer A earned a score of 29 points because her characteristics matched the retailer's ideal profitable customer.

Customer A

Gender: Female	8 points
Amount spent: $100	10 points
Gourmet cooking: yes	5 points
Wines: yes	6 points
Total score:	29 points

Customer B, on the other hand, scored only 7 points because he reflected only two key characteristics on the retailer's scoring system.

Customer B

Gender: male	0 points
Amount spent: $10	1 point
Gourmet cooking: no	0 points
Wines: yes	6 points
Total score:	7 points

Subsequently, the customers who scored in the highest 10 percent of the customer base will form Decile 1 in the gains table. If the weighted points are considered in terms of predicted future profit dollars, then a future profit-based gains table as described earlier can be created. For example, by converting 10 points to $10, 8 points to $8, 5 points to $5, the predicted profit for Customer A is $29 instead of 29 points.

In addition, the individual's score or decile assignment can also be stored in the customer database for future selection and research purposes. Through relationship marketing, marketers may be able to develop an effective strategy to encourage customers to migrate from lower deciles into higher, more profitable deciles.

Using Regression Analysis to Identify the Questions to Ask

In the process of identifying the four relevant predictive questions to ask, the retailer was able to take advantage of a statistical procedure provided by the researcher. The statistical method used in this example is called multiple linear regression analysis.

Regression analysis can be used to generate a mathematical formula that includes a number of significant predictive variables, each multiplied by a different weighting coefficient, to produce an estimated value that will indicate purchase potential. The most important predictive variables are assigned a higher weighting called a *regression coefficient*. In the case of the cookbook retailer, the best predictive variable was spending one hundred dollars on books. This behavior characteristic was then allocated 10 points, the highest weight in the equation.

Readers interested in further information on regression and other statistical analysis can consult any multivariate statistical reference book. It is necessary to point out that building this type of scoring model does require a minimum level of expertise in statistics.

In the scenario described earlier, the role of regression analysis was to identify those questions that are correlated with a customer's future profitability. Often, a marketer will start out with two or three hundred possible predictive variables. Using regression analysis, an experienced researcher can recode and combine various predictive variables, identify the interaction effects, and employ a relatively small number of selected predictive variables to calculate a score that will indicate a customer's future purchase potential. For example, direct marketers found that behavior data such as purchase recency, frequency, monetary value, and category are often quite accurate in predicting who is most likely and least likely to purchase from the subsequent promotion effort. In sum, regression analysis can be used to help identify the right set of questions to ask and to assign relative importance to the answers of these predictive questions.

First Things First: Data Retrieval and Interface

Before performing any statistical analysis, raw data needs to be retrieved, refined, and organized into a format that can be easily processed by an available statistical package such as SPSS or SAS software programs. This data interface process is essential to the success of subsequent query and modeling activities. If the data retrieval process is not easily accessible and user-friendly, those working with the customer database may be frustrated, unwilling to request further analysis, and unenthusiastic about taking full advantage of the database.

In view of these concerns, some companies have begun to create personal computer applications that interface with their mainframe computers. For example, a quick count application can be developed to give managers easy access to customer information at an aggregated level. Alternatively, a secondary, "mini" database of summarized customer statistics can be created to efficiently answer immediate marketing information needs.

Finding Out What You *Do Not* Know

Analysis and modeling can enable database marketers not only to summarize what they already know about their best customers or prospects, but also to learn what they do *not* know about their customers. When a model fails to predict a customer's future behavior, marketers need to ask themselves whether they truly know enough about their customers.

Some organizations find themselves data-rich and information-poor. The process of planning and evaluating database-driven analysis and modeling often can spot a company's information shortage while triggering added ideas for future data collection and research projects.

Validating the Model

The best scoring model is the one that has been tested and validated in the real world. In the process of building models over time, continued tests, adjustments, and improvements help assure that the model is valid.

Repeating the model-building process is the best insurance for checking the viability of predictive models. This enables a marketer to gain an understanding of the changes taking place in the marketplace, add important new variables to the model, and rebuild it according to different situations and the changing competitive environment.

An alternative means to validate the model is to use the split sample method. In this method, half of the sample is randomly selected to build the scoring model, and the other half is reserved for validation purposes. The model is considered to be valid if the regression equation created from the first half of the sample can reasonably predict the behavior of the second half of the sample.

If the model does not perform as anticipated—for example, if it is unable to differentiate meaningfully the profitable and unprofitable customer segments—the failure is not necessarily the result of a faulty model. Statistical methods alone are generally not the primary reason that a model fails.

One common reason for a model's failure is the lack of relevant predictive variables. In other words, the wrong questions have been asked and future behavior cannot reliably be predicted from the information supplied. To overcome this problem, the marketer needs to reexamine the data source strategy and possibly invest resources to identify the right questions to ask.

However, a model can also fail to perform due to inaccurate and unreliable customer data, even if the relevant predictive variables are included. To correct this problem, the data collection process must be reviewed and security systems installed to eliminate mistakes in data entry.

Yet another reason for a model's failure to perform may be an insufficient variance in the dependent variables. In other words, if every customer behaves in exactly the same way, or if the sample used for modeling does not include enough respondents, the scoring model will not be predictive.

The marketer should be informed of how successful the scoring model was and of the reasons for this level of success. Whenever a new model is proposed, a predetermined level of success should be required for that model.

Building Multiple Models

One model will not fit every marketing need. Rather, in certain marketing situations multiple scoring models are required to predict customer behavior and desirable results accurately. For example, an insurance marketer can build a response model to predict customer segments most likely to sign up for the company's policy. On the other hand, those most likely to respond may also have a high tendency to be involved in accidents. Thus, two complementary models may be needed: one to predict response and the other to predict risk and liability. The two models can then be combined to determine the most desirable segments upon which to focus the allocation of marketing resources. Similarly, some companies will use a primary model to predict profitability and a related model to determine the bad-debt tendency among their customers.

Several other types of models are also available to a marketer. For example, an attrition model can be developed to predict whether a customer will continue to do business with a company. A credit card company may use this type of model to determine whether particular customers will cancel their cards or discontinue their services.

The Usable Life of a Scoring Model

Any scoring model has a limited period of effectiveness. The model's life span depends on how quickly the market environment and customer demand change. In a mature product category, conditions change slowly and models have a longer shelf life. However, in a rapidly-changing market such as the high-technology arena, the external environment can change so quickly and unpredictably that models have a much shorter usable life.

In theory, once a scoring model has been completed it is already obsolete. Every model should be revised and adapted to reflect changes in the marketplace.

Analyzing Scoring Model Payoff

A marketer needs to take into account the costs involved in building a scoring model. In general, customized scoring models developed by outside consultants can range from $20,000 to $60,000. The final cost depends upon the nature and complexity of the model as well as the consultant's experience in data analysis. Another cost factor is the level of difficulty in data preparation and retrieval—the more difficult it is to capture and clean data, the less cost effective the model is. In many cases, addressing the problem of data integrity or accuracy will entail additional expense.

As a result, before deciding to build a scoring model, a marketer must reasonably expect to recover development costs. Ideally, the model should pay for itself and provide incremental profits in order to be considered a sound investment. Another fringe benefit that should be considered in building a model is the amount of customer insight a marketer can gain through its development. This knowledge, while not necessarily quantifiable in dollars and cents, should be taken into account when evaluating the total financial investment.

Limitations of Scoring Models

A scoring model is not the answer to every marketing problem. A model cannot compensate for a poor product or for inappropriate marketing decisions. For example, when a financial service company experienced decreased profitability from its credit card operation, database consultants were called in to perform a scoring model that would help the marketers improve their division's profitability by identifying good credit risks.

Unfortunately, after spending nearly $50,000 on the model, the managers still failed to achieve their objective. They then realized that the main cause of the decreased profitability was a high credit-card cancellation rate. After recognizing that the main problem was the company's inability to keep existing customers, managers finally began contacting cardholders who canceled their service directly. They learned that their card charged the highest interest rates while providing the lowest level of service in their market.

The lesson to be learned from this example is that a marketer's job is to create customers. Though they might create scoring models for short-term profit manipulation, this is not a means of creating more customers.

Other Useful Analytical Tools

In order to interpret and manage large amounts of customer information, database marketers need all the help that they can get from analysis and modeling. Researchers need to learn to experiment gradually in order to identify the most appropriate and effective statistical tools for specific marketing applications.

In addition to the predictive models described above, other types of mathematical models developed by marketing scientists can also be adopted to help marketers better understand marketing dynamics and make informed decisions. For example, descriptive models can be used to examine the potential impact of the marketing mix (product, price, place, and promotion) on sales and profit. Prescriptive models can be used to help a marketer solve specific problems, such as inventory or logistical resource allocations.

Today, marketers have access to a variety of software packages, such as spreadsheet and statistical programs. Most spreadsheet programs have a built-in statistical function that can perform simple regression analysis. Statistical packages such as SPSS and SAS are available for both personal and mainframe computers to facilitate more sophisticated data manipulation and statistical analysis.

Commercially available statistical packages generally include procedures for various types of statistical analysis. For example, these programs all have basic data examination procedures, such as descriptive statistics, frequency analysis, missing value, box plot, histogram, and stem-and-leaf analysis. These tools can provide useful information about the range and distribution of a variable. An experienced researcher usually begins by paying attention to small details and carefully examining each variable that goes into a model.

Statistical tools such as analysis of variance (ANOVA) can be used in a testing situation to determine whether the customer performance of the control group is significantly different from that of the treatment group. Cross tabulation and correlation analyses may be used to describe the relationship among various variables.

Advanced statistical tools such as regression analysis, discriminant analysis, logistic regression analysis, and automatic interaction detection (AID/CHAID analysis) are used in the creation of predictive models. Regression analysis is better suited for predicting a customer's future sales or profit potential. Logistic regression analysis is best suited for predicting response to a specific promotion. CHAID can effectively detect interaction effects among variables and can be effectively used in conjunction with regression analysis.

Factor analysis is a useful tool for data reduction. It allows a marketer to summarize a large number of predictive variables into a small number of meaningful factors. These factors, in the form of factor scores, can then be integrated into a regression analysis. Cluster analysis groups customers with similar characteristics into a single segment. For example, geo-demographics analysis would use cluster analysis to categorize people into different subgroups according to the type of area where they live.

Multidimensional scaling analysis, such as ALSCAL, can be used to create perceptual maps. This allows a marketer to examine the strategic positioning of his or her own brand compared to competitors' brands. Conjoint analysis can be employed in order to investigate customer preferences.

Survival analysis and hazard models deal with the time period and occurrence of events, such as repeat purchases. Survival analysis predicts when the next event (for example, purchase, return of goods, or death) will occur.

The availability of large volumes of data has also attracted new technologies such as fractal geometry, neural network, nearest neighbor, and artificial intelligence to the database marketing industry. These new technologies can potentially increase the speed, as well as the power, of database analysis and modeling. However, it is important to point out that marketing decision making should remain largely a managerial task. Statistical and mathematical tools are mainly the means to an end and should never replace a marketer's sound judgment and creative thinking.

A Hypothetical Lifetime Value Model and "What If?" Analysis

Traditionally, companies think of assets as being physical and tangible. Developing this type of asset means investing in new machinery, or expanding merchandise offerings through new product development, and so on. New thinking shows that customers are assets, too. They represent a continuous stream of cash flow from the interaction between the business and the consumer.

All too often, marketing measures its own success by the total number of new customers obtained by an offer or premium or other marketing effort. As the series of models that follows demonstrates, it is, however, more valuable to a business to achieve qualified customers upfront and focus on *retaining* them than it is to constantly search out new customers.

Three customer management objectives are essential to database marketing.

1. Acquire new customers: be selective and pre-qualify your leads.

2. Satisfy those customers: meet their expectations and more—go beyond what they anticipate from both your product and service, making sure that what you provide is relevant.

3. Generate repeat customers: work on the relationship you have with your customers in order to stimulate repeat business. This is a relationship that's worth working on—don't give up too easily, but don't annoy your customers in the process.

In this hypothetical lifetime value model, we assume that we can manipulate the following marketing elements.

Price

- Initial cost to customer
- Price increase: amount and frequency

Promotion

- Use of promotion as a marketing tool
- Type of promotion (discount, gift, and so on)
- Amount of price incentive offered
- Value of gift (cost to company)

Advertising revenue

- Ability to offset expenses with money from advertisers
- Amount

Direct costs

- Cost of goods sold
- Quality of goods and service provided

Renewal efforts

- Use of renewal efforts: number and frequency
- Cost for each renewal effort
- Response to each effort

Relationship marketing efforts

- Use of a relationship-building device as a marketing tool
- Relevance to customers' needs and wants
- Value added to long-term relationship
- Cost
- Impact on response

Timing of revenues

- Customer payments
- Advertising revenue

Timing of expenses

- Direct cost
- Renewal cost
- Relationship marketing cost

Discount rate

- Time value of money
- Return on investment

Initial investment

- Amount spent on recruiting 1,000 new customers
- Method of obtaining new customers

Model A

Table 11-2 presents the first lifetime value model. Currently, our company charges $22 for the product it sells to its customers. For this example, let's say that product is an annual subscription to a magazine or continuity program.

We use promotion to gain new customers. We have been successful using a combination of price incentive and free gift:

- Initial discount is $5
- Gift cost is $5

As a result, net revenue from each customer is $12 for the first year.

We also gain advertising revenue equal to 100 percent of the customer revenue (before discounts and premiums). Our direct costs are 65 percent of total revenue. We produce one renewal mailing each year. It costs $300 per thousand mailed. Response to this renewal effort is 45 percent the first year and 50 percent for each of the following years. This is because we have some deal-prone customers who responded to the initial promotion and are less likely to renew the second year when they would pay full price. We do no other marketing to promote customer loyalty.

Our initial investment to gain these 1,000 customers was $10,000. We need to factor in a discount rate of 20 percent. Customer revenue is received at the beginning of the accounting period and advertising revenue at mid-year. The direct cost is incurred at mid-year and renewal expenses at the end of the year.

The five-year lifetime value for an individual is $12.18.

Table 11-2   Model A

	Year 1	Year 2	Year 3	Year 4	Year 5
New Customers	1,000				
Repeat Customers		450	225	113	56
Retention Rate		45.0%	50.0%	50.0%	50.0%
Revenue					
Price @	$22	$23	$24	$25	$26
Price Incentive @	$5				
Free Gift @	$5				
Net Price @	$12	$23	$24	$25	$26
Total Cust. Revenue	$12,000	$10,350	$5,400	$2,813	$1,463
Discount Rate	1.00	1.20	1.44	1.73	2.07
Total Cust. Revenue (NPV)	$12,000	$8,625	$3,750	$1,628	$705
Ad Revenue @	$22	$23	$24	$25	$26
Total Ad Revenue	$22,000	$10,350	$5,400	$2,813	$1,463
Discount Rate	1.10	1.31	1.58	1.89	2.27
Total Ad Revenue (NPV)	$20,083	$7,874	$3,423	$1,486	$644
Total Revenue (NPV)	$32,083	$16,499	$7,173	$3,113	$1,349
Expenses					
Direct Cost %	65.0%	65.0%	65.0%	65.0%	65.0%
Total Direct Cost	$22,100	$13,455	$7,020	$3,656	$1,901
Discount Rate	1.10	1.31	1.58	1.89	2.27
Total Direct Cost (NPV)	$20,174	$10,236	$4,450	$1,932	$837
Renewal Effort					
Target Customers	1,000	450	225	113	56
Renewal Rate	45.0%	50.0%	50.0%	50.0%	50.0%
Customer Renewals	450	225	113	56	28
Total Customer Renewals	450	225	113	56	28
Total Mailing Quantity	1,000	450	225	113	56
Renewal Cost/M	$300	$300	$300	$300	$300
Total Renewal Cost	$300	$135	$68	$34	$17
Discount Rate	1.20	1.44	1.73	2.07	2.49
Total Renewal Cost (NPV)	$250	$94	$39	$16	$7
Total Expenses (NPV)	$20,424	$10,329	$4,489	$1,948	$844
Contribution (NPV)	$11,659	$6,169	$2,684	$1,166	$505
Initial Investment	$10,000				
Total Lifetime Value	$1,659	$7,828	$10,512	$11,677	$12,183
Individual Lifetime Value	$1.66	$7.83	$10.51	$11.68	$12.18

Model B

But "what if" we didn't use promotion?

Our initial customer revenue is increased by $10,000 ($5,000 saved by not offering the discount; $5,000 saved by eliminating the free gift). As a result, total revenue for the first year is $44,000 (or a net present value of $42,083). Our initial investment to gain these 1,000 customers increases to $15,000. Promotion makes it easier to quickly gain customers. Without the use of promotional incentives, more advertising and mailings are needed to find the same number of customers. This increases the upfront investment needed. Customers are more interested in our product because they were willing to pay full price in the beginning.

Response to the renewal mailing increases to 55 percent during the first year, and then stabilizes at 50 percent during subsequent years. These customers were more qualified through their interest in our product than when heavy initial promotion was used, and thus are most likely to sign up with us for a second year.

The five-year lifetime value for an individual increases to $13.59. It is, therefore, worth eliminating promotion to gain more qualified, and potentially more loyal, customers.

Table 11-3   Model B

	Year 1	Year 2	Year 3	Year 4	Year 5
New Customers	1,000				
Repeat Customers		550	275	138	69
Retention Rate		55.0%	50.0%	50.0%	50.0%
Revenue					
Price @	$22	$23	$24	$25	$26
Price Incentive @	$0				
Free Gift @	$0				
Net Price @	$22	$23	$24	$25	$26
Total Cust. Revenue	$22,000	$12,650	$6,600	$3,438	$1,788
Discount Rate	1.00	1.20	1.44	1.73	2.07
Total Cust. Revenue (NPV)	$22,000	$10,542	$4,583	$1,989	$862
Ad Revenue @	$22	$23	$24	$25	$26
Total Ad Revenue	$22,000	$12,650	$6,600	$3,438	$1,788
Discount Rate	1.10	1.31	1.58	1.89	2.27
Total Ad Revenue (NPV)	$20,083	$9,623	$4,184	$1,816	$787
Total Revenue (NPV)	$42,083	$20,165	$8,767	$3,805	$1,649
Expenses					
Direct Cost %	65.0%	65.0%	65.0%	65.0%	65.0%
Total Direct Cost	$28,600	$16,445	$8,580	$4,469	$2,324
Discount Rate	1.10	1.31	1.58	1.89	2.27
Total Direct Cost (NPV)	$26,108	$12,510	$5,439	$2,361	$1,023
Renewal Effort					
Target Customers	1,000	550	275	138	69
Renewal Rate	55.0%	50.0%	50.0%	50.0%	50.0%
Customer Renewals	550	275	138	69	34
Total Customer Renewals	550	275	138	69	34
Total Mailing Quantity	1,000	550	275	138	69
Renewal Cost/M	$300	$300	$300	$300	$300
Total Renewal Cost	$300	$165	$83	$41	$21
Discount Rate	1.20	1.44	1.73	2.07	2.49
Total Renewal Cost (NPV)	$250	$115	$48	$20	$8
Total Expenses (NPV)	$26,358	$12,625	$5,487	$2,381	$1,031
Contribution (NPV)	$15,725	$7,540	$3,280	$1,425	$618
Initial Investment	$15,000				
Total Lifetime Value	$725	$8,265	$11,546	$12,970	$13,588
Individual Lifetime Value	$0.73	$8.27	$11.55	$12.97	$13.59

Model C

But "what if" we add a second renewal mailing?

We add the expense of sending a second mailing to customers who did not respond to the first effort. Response to this mailing is 15 percent. The five-year lifetime value for an individual increases to $16.37. It is therefore, worth the expense of adding a second renewal mailing to gain the renewed loyalty of these extra customers.

Table 11-4   Model C

	Year 1	Year 2	Year 3	Year 4	Year 5
New Customers	1,000				
Repeat Customers		618	355	204	117
Retention Rate		61.8%	57.5%	57.5%	57.5%
Revenue					
Price @	$22	$23	$24	$25	$26
Price Incentive @	$0				
Free Gift @	$0				
Net Price @	$22	$23	$24	$25	$26
Total Cust. Revenue	$22,000	$14,203	$8,522	$5,104	$3,052
Discount Rate	1.00	1.20	1.44	1.73	2.07
Total Cust. Revenue (NPV)	$22,000	$11,835	$5,918	$2,954	$1,472
Ad Revenue @	$22	$23	$24	$25	$26
Total Ad Revenue	$22,000	$14,203	$8,522	$5,104	$3,052
Discount Rate	1.10	1.31	1.58	1.89	2.27
Total Ad Revenue (NPV)	$20,083	$10,804	$5,402	$2,696	$1,344
Total Revenue (NPV)	$42,083	$22,640	$11,320	$5,650	$2,816
Expenses					
Direct Cost %	65.0%	65.0%	65.0%	65.0%	65.0%
Total Direct Cost	$28,600	$18,463	$11,078	$6,635	$3,968
Discount Rate	1.10	1.31	1.58	1.89	2.27
Total Direct Cost (NPV)	$26,108	$14,045	$7,023	$3,505	$1,747
Renewal Effort 1					
Target Customers	1,000	618	355	204	117
Renewal Rate	55.0%	50.0%	50.0%	50.0%	50.0%
Customer Renewals	550	309	178	102	59
Renewal Effort 2					
Target Customers	450	309	178	102	59
Renewal Rate	15.0%	15.0%	15.0%	15.0%	15.0%
Customer Renewals	68	46	27	15	9
Total Customer Renewals	618	355	204	117	68
Total Mailing Quantity	1,450	926	533	306	176
Renewal Cost/M	$300	$300	$300	$300	$300
Total Renewal Cost	$435	$278	$160	$92	$53
Discount Rate	1.20	1.44	1.73	2.07	2.49
Total Renewal Cost (NPV)	$363	$193	$92	$44	$21
Total Expenses (NPV)	$26,471	$14,238	$7,115	$3,550	$1,768
Contribution (NPV)	$15,613	$8,401	$4,205	$2,101	$1,048
Initial Investment	$15,000				
Total Lifetime Value	$613	$9,014	$13,218	$15,319	$16,366
Individual Lifetime Value	$0.61	$9.01	$13.22	$15.32	$16.37

Model D

But "what if" we added a third renewal mailing?

We add the expense of sending another mailing to customers who did not respond to the first or second effort. Response to this mailing is five percent.

The five-year lifetime value for an individual increases to $17.10. Despite the small percentage of renewals gained and the added cost, it is still worthwhile for us to implement a third mailing to retain these additional customers.

Table 11-5   Model D

	Year 1	Year 2	Year 3	Year 4	Year 5
New Customers	1,000				
Repeat Customers		637	380	226	135
Retention Rate		63.7%	59.6%	59.6%	59.6%
Revenue					
Price @	$22	$23	$24	$25	$26
Price Incentive @	$0				
Free Gift @	$0				
Net Price @	$22	$23	$24	$25	$26
Total Cust. Revenue	$22,000	$14,642	$9,110	$5,658	$3,509
Discount Rate	1.00	1.20	1.44	1.73	2.07
Total Cust. Revenue (NPV)	$22,000	$12,202	$6,326	$3,274	$1,692
Ad Revenue @	$22	$23	$24	$25	$26
Total Ad Revenue	$22,000	$14,642	$9,110	$5,658	$3,509
Discount Rate	1.10	1.31	1.58	1.89	2.27
Total Ad Revenue (NPV)	$20,083	$11,139	$5,775	$2,989	$1,545
Total Revenue (NPV)	$42,083	$23,341	$12,102	$6,264	$3,237
Expenses					
Direct Cost %	65.0%	65.0%	65.0%	65.0%	65.0%
Total Direct Cost	$28,600	$19,035	$11,843	$7,356	$4,561
Discount Rate	1.10	1.31	1.58	1.89	2.27
Total Direct Cost (NPV)	$26,108	$14,480	$7,508	$3,886	$2,008
Renewal Effort 1					
Target Customers	1,000	637	380	226	135
Renewal Rate	55.0%	50.0%	50.0%	50.0%	50.0%
Customer Renewals	550	318	190	113	67
Renewal Effort 2					
Target Customers	450	318	190	113	67
Renewal Rate	15.0%	15.0%	15.0%	15.0%	15.0%
Customer Renewals	68	48	28	17	10
Renewal Effort 3					
Target Customers	383	271	161	96	57
Renewal Rate	5.0%	5.0%	5.0%	5.0%	5.0%
Customer Renewals	19	14	8	5	3
Total Customer Renewals	637	380	226	135	80
Total Mailing Quantity	1,833	1,226	731	436	260
Renewal Cost/M	$300	$300	$300	$300	$300
Total Renewal Cost	$550	$368	$219	$131	$78
Discount Rate	1.20	1.44	1.73	2.07	2.49
Total Renewal Cost (NPV)	$458	$255	$127	$63	$31
Total Expenses (NPV)	$26,566	$14,736	$7,635	$3,949	$2,039
Contribution (NPV)	$15,517	$8,605	$4,467	$2,315	$1,197
Initial Investment	$15,000				
Total Lifetime Value	$517	$9,122	$13,589	$15,904	$17,101
Individual Lifetime Value	$0.52	$9.12	$13.59	$15.90	$17.10

Model E

But "what if" we added a relationship marketing effort?

The cost for developing and producing this marketing tool is $500 per 1,000 customers—substantially more than for the standard renewal mailing efforts. This mailing is sent to all customers who have paid their annual amount before the three renewal mailings are sent out. This relationship marketing effort successfully ties into the interests of the company's customers. Customers who continue to receive this extra item each year have a high level of loyalty towards the company and its product.

The increase in customer loyalty leads to an increase in response to the series of three renewal mailings. As this loyalty builds over the five-year period, each renewal mailing generates an increase of just one percent in response. For example, response during the first year to the three mailings is 55 percent, 15 percent and 5 percent, respectively. When the marketing plan includes this relationship-building tool, response increases to 56 percent, 16 percent and 6 percent during the same period. The second-year response climbs to 57 percent, 17 percent and 7 percent, and so forth.

The five-year lifetime value for an individual reaches $17.52. This additional loyalty-building effort, despite the high $500 per thousand cost, is an important and viable stage in our company's long-term marketing strategy.

Table 11-6   Model E

	Year 1	Year 2	Year 3	Year 4	Year 5
New Customers	1,000				
Repeat Customers		653	411	265	175
Retention Rate		65.3%	62.9%	64.5%	66.1%
Revenue					
Price @	$22	$23	$24	$25	$26
Price Incentive @	$0				
Free Gift @	$0				
Net Price @	$22	$23	$24	$25	$26
Total Cust. Revenue	$22,000	$15,009	$9,859	$6,628	$4,556
Discount Rate	1.00	1.20	1.44	1.73	2.07
Total Cust. Revenue (NPV)	$22,000	$12,508	$6,846	$3,836	$2,197
Ad Revenue @	$22	$23	$24	$25	$26
Total Ad Revenue	$22,000	$15,009	$9,859	$6,628	$4,556
Discount Rate	1.10	1.31	1.58	1.89	2.27
Total Ad Revenue (NPV)	$20,083	$11,418	$6,250	$3,502	$2,006
Total Revenue (NPV)	$42,083	$23,926	$13,096	$7,338	$4,203
Expenses					
Direct Cost %	65.0%	65.0%	65.0%	65.0%	65.0%
Total Direct Cost	$28,600	$19,512	$12,817	$8,617	$5,923
Discount Rate	1.10	1.31	1.58	1.89	2.27
Total Direct Cost (NPV)	$26,108	$14,843	$8,125	$4,552	$2,608
Renewal Effort 1					
Target Customers	1,000	653	411	265	175
Renewal Rate	56.0%	52.0%	53.0%	54.0%	55.0%
Customer Renewals	560	339	218	143	96
Renewal Effort 2					
Target Customers	440	313	193	122	79
Renewal Rate	16.0%	17.0%	18.0%	19.0%	20.0%
Customer Renewals	70	53	35	23	16
Renewal Effort 3					
Target Customers	370	260	158	99	63
Renewal Rate	6.0%	7.0%	8.0%	9.0%	10.0%
Customer Renewals	22	18	13	9	6
Total Customer Renewals	653	411	265	175	118
Total Mailing Quantity	1,810	1,226	762	486	317
Renewal Cost/M	$300	$300	$300	$300	$300
Total Renewal Cost	$543	$368	$229	$146	$95
Discount Rate	1.20	1.44	1.73	2.07	2.49
Total Renewal Cost (NPV)	$452	$255	$132	$70	$38
Relationship Marketing Effort					
Target Customers	1,000	653	411	265	175
Marketing Cost/M	$500	$500	$500	$500	$500
Total Marketing Cost	$500	$326	$205	$133	$88
Discount Rate	1.10	1.31	1.58	1.89	2.27
Total Marketing Cost (NPV)	$456	$248	$130	$70	$39
Total Expenses (NPV)	$27,017	$15,347	$8,387	$4,692	$2,684
Contribution (NPV)	$15,066	$8,579	$4,709	$2,645	$1,519
Initial Investment	$15,000				
Total Lifetime Value	$66	$8,645	$13,354	$15,999	$17,518
Individual Lifetime Value	$0.07	$8.64	$13.35	$16.00	$17.52

Lifetime Value Is a Critical Measurement of Success

To reiterate, customers are important assets to a business. Lifetime value is a critical measurement of success. Using lifetime value as a key consideration in all planning and implementation of marketing strategy is increasingly becoming "a way of doing business."

Lifetime value helps a company's marketing and financial divisions work together towards a common, customer-oriented goal. Unfortunately, individuals on both the marketing and financial ends often fail to take into account each other's goals. The concept of lifetime value enables the idea-generators to quantify the results of their marketing plan so that the number-crunchers can evaluate its ultimate financial benefit to the company. It must be remembered that the payback is long-term, so total organizational commitment is imperative for success.

Lifetime value models *can* be based only on historical data. However, this method limits the marketing effort. Not only should a marketer look at past history when preparing a lifetime value model, but he or she should continually evaluate their strategy in light of its ultimate relevance and added value to the customer.

Identifying Research Needs by Point of Entry into Database Marketing

Now, you have an understanding of the value of segmentation and research, the last of the three key building blocks for database marketing. To translate this information to your database marketing requirements, you must conduct your own analysis of appropriate research and segmentation techniques. Once completed, use the matrix in Figure 11-1 to equate your research requirements to the three points of entry into database marketing. The matrix illustrates with Xs the types of data usually found in marketing databases associated with each point of entry. This exercise, when combined with similar analysis of your requirements for the other key building blocks of database marketing, will provide insight into your overall entry point and requirements for development of your marketing database.

Figure 11-1   Research and Segmentation Decision Matrix

	Point of Entry		
	Historical Data Management	Marketing Intelligence	Integrated Resource
Research Type			
Customer Profiles	X	X	X
Customer Segmentation Recency/ Frequency/Monetary Value	X	X	X
Predictive Customer Modeling/Scoring		X	X
Predictive Prospect Modeling/Scoring		X	X
Product/Purchase Segmentation		X	X
Offer Segmentation		X	X
Characteristic Segmentation		X	X
Strategic Segmentation			X

Conclusion

Even when they allocated millions of dollars to collect customer data and build sophisticated relational databases, some companies still fail to invest the time and resources necessary to completely plan and organize their statistical analysis and modeling functions. Lacking this analysis and modeling capacity is likely to limit a marketer's ability to take full advantage of the existing database. When marketers begin to understand and appreciate the value of statistical analysis, they are more likely to make the right decisions in allocating appropriate research resources.

Note

1. Andreasen, Alan R. "Backward Marketing Research," *Harvard Business Review,* May/ June 1985.

P A R T

IV

Managing
the Database

C H A P T E R **12**

Putting Together Your Database Marketing System

The whole is greater than the sum of its parts.

This may be the most important chapter in this book. Here we discuss the process that brings our methodology together with the information you need to begin defining and implementing your own marketing database.

After reading to this point, you have a marketer's view of the three key database building blocks of data, technology, and statistical techniques. You also should have an understanding of data-driven marketing applications. Now it is time to attempt to define your own database marketing needs with the unique combination of resources that make sense for your marketing applications and business requirements.

Plan Applications before Technology

The "walls" of your database "house" are the applications your database will perform. The applications serve as the parameters or boundaries for your marketing database. You must therefore determine the appropriate applications before you can go forward with your effort. Understanding your applications will help you to determine what combination of resources is necessary for your marketing database. Remember this key principle: *applications before technology.* Even if you ultimately decide to use a packaged database product . . . start at the beginning. Understand your marketing applications and corresponding resource requirements first. Then you can make an intelligent decision on the trade-offs you are making and the limitations of the systems you build.

Plotting Your Point of Entry

Once you have determined your unique set of database applications, it is time to apply them to the database methodology to build the blueprint for your marketing database. You may find it helpful at this point to review the marketing database case histories that were presented in Chapter 6, or the major data-driven marketing applications described in Chapter 4. Each case history was presented along the database continuum of historical data management, marketing information system, and integrated business resource.

The goal of this process is to plot your application along the continuum of database applications and then match your application with the decision criteria and combination of key building blocks necessary to accomplish your objectives.

Developing your database applications requires a good deal of thinking beyond the obvious. It is easy to say that our objective is to sell our product via targeted direct mail. But this is not a database application. It is a communications tactic generated by a database marketing application. Remember, a marketing database is a key strategic resource for your business and a long-term marketing tool. To be successful, you must construct your database applications as the basis of a customer-based strategy. For example, the following are a few strategic objectives of database marketing programs:

- Customer retention
- Information search facilitation
- Customer relationship management
- Sales maximization
- New customer development
- Research
- Communications effectiveness measurement
- Development of new distribution channels
- Communications management
- Plus many, many others

We are not against thinking about tactics. In fact, you must consider them. However, you must view your database resource strategically first, then translate each strategic objective into a list of tactics that the database can drive.

For example, your strategy could be to cross-sell your products, and your tactic to model your best customers, segment your database accordingly, and then communicate with your best customers through direct mail or telemarketing.

Once you have set your strategic course and placed parameters around your database applications, you can focus on tactical execution of your strategic objectives that a database can support. At this point, you should be able to take two actions we have explored in this book. First, plot your data-driven application along the continuum of applications (see Figure 8-10, page 134), and second, chart your application along the point-of-entry decision matrix in Table 3-1 (pp. 32–37).

By plotting your application along the continuum, you are starting the process of mapping your resource requirements. Each point along the continuum requires a different combination of the key building blocks to support your applications. From this point of entry into data-driven marketing, you can now examine the point-of-entry decision matrix for your application (Figure 3-1).

The point-of-entry decision was discussed in Chapter 3. The decision matrix has five sections: marketing requirements, organizational requirements, information management requirements, technology requirements, and financial requirements. Under each of the five headings are descriptions of how a database might function for each requirement. Put an "X" in the column of the description that makes the most sense for your business situation. This will allow you to gain a preliminary understanding of the areas of your organization and the areas of consideration that will be affected by your database development decision.

From this analysis, you may decide to develop your application in a multiphased approach. For example, you may decide that for resource conservation, you should start at a point of entry in historical data management and advance up the continuum to marketing intelligence over a two- or three-year period. Plan this process as a series of phases and review the resources required for each phase independently.

This concludes phase 1 of the marketing database development process. At the end of this phase, you should have an understanding of the business implications and considerations that relate to your database effort. In addition, your application should be plotted along the continuum of applications and a point of entry or a phased series of entry points established. If you need help in this process, visit experts, hire a consultant, or form a committee. Get comfortable with your goals and the resulting resource commitments and implementation schedule.

Analyzing Your Application's Requirements

In phase 2 of the marketing database development process, you will proceed to detailed analysis of the requirements for data technology and statistical techniques associated with your application. We have provided in-depth information on the importance and nature of each element and how they relate to each point of entry on the database continuum. The matrices at the end of Chapter 7 on source data strategy and Chapter 11 on analysis and modeling allow you to plot your own requirements.

Analysis of technology considerations (Chapters 8 and 9) is the most complicated. It is hard to fit your technology requirements into a nice little box. In addition, with changing technologies and hardware and software advances, every six months that goes by offers new options for database marketers. You may need to rely on a consultant or technology provider to help you through the technology options maze. In Chapter 9, in the section "Point of Entry and Your Database Technology Decision" (page 155) we have provided a summary of technology options for historical data management, marketing information systems, and integrated business resources. Use this as a guide in making your technical resource decision.

Chapters 10 and 11 discuss statistical research options and opportunities. Compare these options with your organization's research requirements.

At the end of phase two, you will have conducted a detailed analysis of your requirements for each of the three key building blocks. Consolidate the results of your analyses into an overview of your investigation. This process will provide insight into where your total requirements fit into the continuum of applications. Usually, at this point, marketing organizations must sit back and reconcile the analysis they have conducted. Technological considerations may lead to one conclusion, research needs to another, communications needs to yet another, and the ultimate tie-breaker, financial limitations, may be blocking the path. Through a facilitation process, you can come to an agreement on a database roadmap that will make sense for your current requirements as well as accommodate future needs.

Developing a Blueprint for Your Database

Phase 3 is the development of a formal plan or blueprint for your marketing database. We will discuss this process in Chapter 13. The analyses presented in this book and the marketing applications continuum provide good illustrations of the business and marketing considerations involved in database development. You are welcome to include them in the presentation of your marketing database plan.

One last word: remember the Great Database Marketing Paradox . . . technology is only one of the three building blocks of a marketing database. Your database will be a valuable resource only if you also commit to the development of data and research. It is better to wait a year to start the process than to implement a plan that is destined to fail because of lack of the foundation necessary for success.

C H A P T E R 13

Selling the Database Marketing Program to Management

So, you, like, walk into your senior manager's office, see. And, like, you say: "You know, we, like need one of those marketing databases. Like, you know. And see, it'll only cost us about $400,000 or $500,000 or so. You know. But, like, we realllly, realllly need it. So, like, what do you say?"

After your manager picks her/himself up off the floor, the reply is: "Oh sure, go ahead. Invest a half a mil with no payout. No problem." . . . NOT. To which you reply: "Bummer."

The Valley Approach to Selling Database

Once you have analyzed your company's database marketing options, the next step is to approach your management with a strategic plan to test data-driven marketing value for your business and a comprehensive plan for development and management of a database that will become a major marketing resource for your company's future. Because the development of a marketing database and data-driven marketing programs represent a huge investment, most business organizations want an opportunity to walk before they run—the chance to test the value of targeted marketing before agreeing to a multiyear commitment of data, technology, research, and marketing support.

Three Ways to Demonstrate the Value of Database Marketing

There are a number of ways to sell data-driven marketing to your management. They include: developing a two-building-block test program, building a prototype or pilot program, and developing a strategic plan.

Developing a Two-Building-Block Test Program

The two key building blocks to the test are data and research. By carefully crafting a test program, you can prove the value of data-driven marketing through implementation of communications programs. We have observed test programs conducted against two segments of a marketer's target audience, the best or most important customer segment and a poorly performing customer segment. The logic of both choices is simple. First, if you can produce incremental gain over past performance for your best customer segment, the rest should be easy. Second, if you can produce improved results from a poorly producing target audience segment, the database will also produce value from higher performing segments. We suggest that by conducting a two-segment test on best and worst performing segments, you will be able to demonstrate the success of data-driven marketing programs at both ends of the customer spectrum, thus proving the value of data-driven marketing over an array of communications requirements.

You will notice that we have not included technology in this test. The emphasis here is on customer relationship improvement rather than on a technical database structure. Once you have proven performance with the test, it will be easier to address the technological issues.

Core to the test is to have a file or list of the target audience segments for which you wish to demonstrate improved performance. This list should have trackable responses from the last communications effort or efforts. In other words, you must be able to identify who you targeted and who did and did not respond. Now, with the help of a research analyst, you can overlay external enhancement data, if necessary, and then build a response or segmentation model attempting to understand the differences between nonresponders and buyers. In addition, it will be beneficial to develop a lifetime value model on high responders. It is important also to understand their relationship to your business and products—in other words, how and why they buy from you.

The output from this research process will take two forms. For the low-producing end of your customer file or target audience, you will have developed a model that will either identify how to reduce your mailing and gain the same response or how to increase your response with the same mailing size. At the high end, you will have learned the buying behavior of your best customers and how best to communicate with them. For example, if you identify repeat purchases in only one product category, you may try a cross-sell approach. If customers buy only on promotion, you may not want to send a full-price offer. If customers are frequent purchasers with a high value over time, you will want to recognize this behavior and reward it.

Once you have results from your test communications programs, analyze them to validate your models, scores, and segmentation programs. At this point you can provide a report to management tracking the short-term gains and the cost to obtain those gains. You can also project lifetime values for long-term customer behavior. At this point, if your tests were successful, you can develop a proforma integrating other long-term data-driven marketing costs such as technology and data access into the equation. The result will be a proof of performance and a realistic cost structure for proceeding with a full data-driven marketing program.

Building a Prototype or Pilot Program

Given the large investment, many organizations wish to take a further step by integrating all three building blocks into a prototype program. The prototype program is a subset of the actual roll-out program. It should perform in every way as you have envisioned the roll-out data-driven marketing program will work. The prototype database can be constructed from an extract of the total database or with a subset of the total universe such as a sales region, group of retail stores, best customers, or sales from your last catalog program.

The advantage of a prototype or pilot program is that the marketer can develop a fully functional system from which to evaluate the functionality of the system and the ongoing costs of the system. In the fully functional prototype, each component of the database system is tested and measured. The disadvantage of this method is cost and timing. Prototype systems will cost almost as much as development of the full database and take proportionally as long to build. The development of prototype systems involves the entire process described in the preceding sections of this book, including development of source data, technology, and statistical techniques.

Source Data

For the prototype, you may not have the time or resources to implement a full source data strategy. However, all types of source data to be represented in the roll-out database must be represented in the pilot program.

Technology

The prototype database may or may not be the full platform and software solution of the roll-out database. If a relational database structure is suggested for the roll-out database, the prototype usually can be conducted in the same relational structure. Often, a pilot program can be developed in a modified version of the design and program structure developed for the roll-out database. Then, if successful, various fine-tuning activities such as final report development, user-friendly access mechanisms, and other data access and counting functions are added in the roll-out phase. If you choose the pilot or prototype program approach, make sure that you document the differences between the test and roll-out.

Statistical Techniques

Crucial to success of your program are statistical research techniques. You must integrate the same research application in the test program as in the roll-out. For example, if scoring models are critical for ongoing success, this activity should be simulated in the pilot program.

Lastly, you must conduct communications or other applications programs just as you would conduct them in a roll-out situation. At the end of the test or evaluation period, you can provide a detailed report to management that reflects the objectives, results, and payout from the test. This report will serve to provide the justification and incentive for development of the roll-out system.

Developing a Strategic Plan

Development of a strategic plan need not be exclusive of a two-building-block or prototype test. In each situation, a plan must be developed that details the objectives, performance, and payout for management. However, in many cases, development of a professional strategic plan without any demonstration is enough to sell a database marketing program to management. The strategic plan alone can provide management with a persuasive argument for the value of the resource. A strategic plan usually includes the eleven elements outlined in the following sections.

Management or Executive Summary

The plan usually begins with an executive summary, a traditional summary of the key factors, analysis, and decisions made or proposed in the document. This section is usually five to ten pages long.

Goals and Objectives

The second section, goals and objectives, represents the realistic expectations that you place upon the proposed system. We suggest that this be presented in terms of the applications continuum and integration of the three key building blocks of data, technology, and research. For tactical databases, the goals will be relative short-term; for relationship databases, goals must be presented in both macro and micro terms. Goals and objectives can be presented in phases that relate to development options. For example, many databases are developed along phased timelines, with various levels of sophistication and applications added in from one to five phases in from one to three years of development.

Situation Analysis

The third section, situation analysis, reviews your current data-driven marketing applications and your future expectations. It can be presented in terms of a gap analysis, which compares the current situation to expectations and reports the gap or difference as the change requirements of the system. The gap analysis can be satisfied in one or several phases of development.

Competitive Analysis

The fourth section reviews both current and future competition by their existing applications and opportunity for competitive initiative. Include analysis of the competitive advantage your business may gain over competition through development of data-driven marketing techniques.

Applications Plan

The fifth section, the applications plan, reviews the marketing applications that will be required by the database and, if appropriate, their phased development. It allows management to gain insight into all the benefits of data-driven marketing for your organization by including an itemized list of the applications' features, benefits, and the goals and objectives the applications can help your business attain.

Operational Plan

The sixth section, the operational plan, details how you will reach your data-driven marketing goals. It reviews each of the key building block areas and details the implementation plans for the organization. Again, this plan is presented in terms of the applications continuum and possibly in phases. In this section, outside resource considerations are presented as a means of plan goal attainment.

Payout Analysis

The seventh section, payout analysis, details the micro and macro marketing return on investment. This can be expressed in terms of responses, sales, or customer value over time. The analysis will support the applications of both short-term tactical programs and long-term relationship programs. All analysis is expressed in terms of customer and sales value.

Financial Analysis

The eighth section, financial analysis, is the traditional accounting review of the business investment. It may take the form of a proforma or show the return on investment for the corporation. It includes the financial implications of section seven.

Requirements

The ninth section, requirements, represents the many resource and other requirements your business must evaluate in terms of implementation of the program. This includes manpower, hardware, software, internal or external design and development, technology advances over time, financial payout timeframes, business investment considerations, and any other factors that relate to your business.

Timelines

The tenth section, timelines, represents the implementation schedule for the data-driven marketing program. The timelines may include side-by-side program development or running periods as well as phased implementation.

Key Next Steps

The eleventh section outlines the key next steps that will move the project forward through the maze of proofs and procedures to expedite development of the program.

Development of a strategic plan may include involvement of outside resources for the following areas: strategic applications advice; technical expertise for hardware, software, and data access requirements; data overlay or enhancement; research applications, or internal versus external development and management. If your evaluations include use of outside resources for applications consulting or external development and management of a system, it is wise to include these resources in the development and presentation of the final plan.

Financial return on investment (ROI) techniques are also crucial to the acceptance of your proposal by management. The following sections discuss the role of ROI in data-driven marketing and outline applicable ROI techniques.

The Leap of Faith and Return on Investment

More times than not, a plan to develop a marketing database is sold to management based more on faith than on a proforma detailing a measurable return on capital investment. And without a doubt, developing a marketing database represents quite a resource commitment.

This leap of faith is one of the most mystifying parts of the database puzzle that we have run into in our database marketing activity. Businesspeople who ordinarily would demand cost estimates and financial analysis plans for any major investment accept a marketing database investment without hard payback numbers.

The reason many marketers rely on a good faith decision is that there is no simple technique or methodology to evaluate whether a database will pay out as a business investment. As each business situation is unique, so is each payout. This lack of standard return-on-investment (ROI) analysis for a marketing database tends to occur for one of two reasons: first, the value of a database is difficult to determine until the database is established, and second, because database development is an art as well as a science.

You Cannot Figure It Out until You Get There

The essence of database marketing is a dialog or relationship between the customer and marketer. While most marketers agree that customer relationships are crucial to future marketing, few marketers can place a financial value on a customer relationship until they have actually reached that point and observed the nature of the relationship with a customer and the payout. Understanding the correct mix of data, technology, statistics, and communications necessary to maximize a relationship marketing program is still uncharted water. In fact, it has not yet been proven that a database is an effective tool for all products, services, or business categories.

Database Development Is an Art as Well as a Science

Development of a database is still at least as much art as science. Two different providers of database technology will develop completely different solutions—and both may be correct. As most marketers who have developed a database will attest, the solution you end up with can be completely different than where you thought you were going based upon matching reality with technology and your specific application.

Two Traps in Database Development

To view a database as a necessary investment, without evaluating the cost of that investment, can create two fatal traps that may doom a database marketing effort to failure from a senior management perspective. The first trap is The Great Database Marketing Paradox, in which marketers focus their attention only on the costs of technology and staffing. They build sophisticated database engines and then expect that they can push a button and relationship marketing programs or predictive consumer behavior scores will pop out of the computer. They then underestimate the funds needed to maximize the data in the database or to obtain the statistical skills to create value from the data. Thus, management eventually has the perspective that they are continually feeding more money into the database machine and not getting a maximization of return.

The second trap is that management often has no benchmark by which to evaluate the return on database investment. Many financial managers see a stream of money flowing to the database with no tangible way to attach a value to the return provided by the database. This will doom any effort over the long term.

To be successful at database-driven marketing, there must be a vision for success—a goal that the database is expected to achieve. This goal or definition of success can be translated into measurable criteria. Thus, ROI represents measurable success compared to the cost to achieve that success. An organization can determine its ROI in terms of alternative use of the resources required to develop the database or against the goals set to measure the success of the effort. Further, the measure of success can be limited strictly to the ability of the database to accomplish the stated objective, or it can include the increase in overall profitability caused by customer management.

Calculating Return on Investment for Your Marketing Database Effort

Three categories of ROI techniques applicable to marketing database efforts are performance analysis, traditional accounting analysis, and economic analysis.

Performance Analysis

Performance analysis techniques review the database investment before a commitment is made to develop the database. Techniques include developing a working prototype and financial simulation.

Working Prototype

A working prototype is a functional subset of the database. It is designed to function as the master or roll-out database would function. A prototype will allow measurement of functional improvements implemented with the database over previous or current methods. It also allows for evaluation and refinement of important applications as the marketer learns "on-the-job" about how the database can be used. ROI is measured in terms of functionality, performance, and cost management. The drawback of this technique is that it is expensive and may be applicable only to larger database marketers. If you do not have a database, a prototype allows you to evaluate inside or outside suppliers and the value of a system at the same time. Given the major resource commitment required by database marketing, the prototype method of evaluation of a potential system will become more common. The prototype system allows you to evaluate both system functionality and customer value payback at the same time. Modeling and revenue techniques such as long-term value analysis should be built into the prototype test.

Financial Simulation

A financial simulation is literally a mathematical model of the functionality of a database. It allows modeling of performance and costs by function, such as various access methods, extracts, models, and enhancement data. Simulation is limited by the ability to gather accurate financial information on costs. Thus the ROI can only be calculated theoretically. However, if you cannot justify a database prototype, financial simulation is useful for evaluation of database functionality as well as customer value payback analysis.

Traditional Accounting Analysis

A database investment can also be reviewed in terms of traditional accounting techniques. This method involves evaluating the database as a major capital investment or as a controllable asset. Techniques include fixed asset analysis and controllable margin analysis.

Fixed Asset Analysis

Fixed asset analysis treats the database as a key strategic asset of the company. It assumes a sophisticated ability to track the array of costs associated with development, management, and access to the database. These costs are weighed against the benefit of the database in terms of sales. The technique assigns an economic life to the database (usually five years) and annualizes the costs to update and refresh the database. Fixed asset analysis measures ROI in terms of net income over the value of the database. This technique ignores the value of a customer. Thus, the asset value of a database does not reflect the difference between a customer with value over time and a sale as a single event. It also does not focus on the functionality of the system.

Controllable Margin Analysis

Controllable margin analysis treats the database as a tactical asset. Financial tracking is limited to database-driven programs. ROI compares controllable costs to sales generated directly by database efforts. This method also ignores customer value over time and focuses on the asset value of a tactical marketing resource. Functionality analysis is also ignored.

Economic Analysis

Economic analysis techniques evaluate performance of an ongoing database in terms of goal attainment or value of the resource to manage customer relationships. Techniques include lifetime value analysis and goal measurement.

Lifetime Value Analysis

Variations of traditional lifetime value analysis (LTV) can provide great insight into various aspects of database programs. For example, LTV can be used to analyze new customer development programs and customer marketing programs. ROI is measured in terms of short- and/or long-term growth of the database. This methodology does take into account the value of a customer over time. Further, it allows "what-if" analysis to simulate changes in promotion, customer acquisition, and other marketing program applications. Lifetime analysis is one of the most powerful techniques available to evaluate customers and their change in value based upon your interaction with them. Do not underestimate this technique just because it has been around since the beginning of direct marketing.

Success Measurement

The success measurement technique works well in analysis of a working database where it is acceptable to measure success in terms of goal attainment rather than traditional financial evaluation. Success measurement techniques compare performance to goals. ROI is evaluated in terms of qualitative or quantitative goal attainment. Success measurement techniques can be used to evaluate both functionality and customer value payback.

ROI and the Application Continuum

In reality, database ROI evaluation usually depends on the nature of the marketing communications application and the complexity of the marketing communications process. As a rule of thumb, the level of evaluation of ROI increases as the sophistication of the application increases. For example, databases at the lower end of the technological continuum are used primarily for tactical applications and drive multimedia communications programs. Cases in this category could include most consumer products databases, in which data is generated from sources such as magazines, television, inserts, co-ops, and in-store methods, but applications are limited to delivery of coupons via direct mail. Databases used in this manner measure success based upon tactical activities such as delivery of promotion via direct mail, not by the long-term ROI to the business.

As the application increases in sophistication to a marketing information system, the value of the database to the organization starts to become strategic as well as tactical. Examples include banks with cross-sell efforts and business-to-business applications with lead qualifications and tiered response based upon sales potential. Databases in this category attempt to predict consumer behavior for prospecting, cross-sell, and upgrade programs and so on. Thus, applications can be evaluated both tactically for program success and with ROI techniques to measure strategic success.

Integrated business resource database systems, at the far end of the continuum, are by nature strategic resources. Applications tend to be limited to direct mail. Examples include mail-order companies and insurance and warranty programs. Databases in this category are always evaluated in terms of return on investment, because without the database, the business could not function.

The bottom line is that the more strategic the application, the more often ROI payback techniques are used both for functional analysis and to calculate customer value payback. We suggest that some combination of ROI techniques are crucial to the success of any database system. Whether your application is tactical or strategic, you want to know that you are getting the best value for your money both functionally and from a customer value standpoint. If a customer contact marketing application is your goal (see Chapter 14), you will find using ROI on an ongoing basis a must.

In summary, few database marketing efforts are evaluated as business investments. Those that are tend to be applications that are strategic in orientation and drive limited multimedia applications. However, the techniques described above can be used for all marketing databases. Some can be used before a commitment is made to develop a database, others can be used to evaluate an existing system.

Whichever technique makes sense for your business situation, all databases are based upon a vision for success. That success translates to measurable activity that can be used for ROI analysis. Evaluation can then be based upon an alternative resource allocation or attainment of a specific goal or success.

Three Case Histories

The following case histories are examples of how different organizations accomplished the process of selling database marketing programs to their management. The three applications we have chosen are a consumer products marketer testing a historical data management database, a major retailer testing a marketing intelligence database, and an insurance marketer testing an integrated business resource database. The names have been withheld and the situation analysis altered to protect the strategic advantage of each of the three organizations.

Corporate and Manager Buy-In in a Consumer Products Company

The organization in this example is a large, multicategory brand marketing and manufacturing company. It is traditionally organized in brand groups responsible for product marketing and promotion. A senior manager over many brand groups became interested in database marketing as a stealth communications tool and a promotion delivery vehicle for several of the manufacturer's highly niched brands. A director of database marketing was hired, reporting to the sales promotion group. The database marketing director developed a financial and operations proforma for capturing and consolidating various promotion files' generation of survey data for a one-year period. This information was incorporated into a presentation that was developed for each brand group. The presentation defined data-driven marketing, the opportunities for the brand groups, costs, and payouts. Each group, with backing of top management, agreed to fund its share of the program.

The director of database marketing then hired an outside vendor to consolidate over 200 files of names and addresses from various promotions, survey programs, and other customer programs generated by the organization over a three-year period. In addition, the brands contracted to gather category and brand-specific users' names via several survey programs. Six months into the program, a master file was developed containing past promotional responses consolidated by household and purchase behavior by household from survey data. The promotion group then developed a series of relationship, cross-sell, micromarketing, and frequency programs based upon the database. The success of the test program during the second six months generated the following conclusions:

- Targeted promotional delivery was more effective on a net purchase basis than FSI delivery both by response and cost per activity
- Strategic value was gained from grouping brands for cross-sell
- Providing sales support to national accounts helped the sales force and provided goodwill for retailer relationships

At the end of the first year, the successful results were delivered to the brand groups in several ways. First, a presentation was made showing brand and corporate success with the program. Second, each brand group received hard-copy and spreadsheet data that allowed them to visualize the power of the database. The brand groups had participated in the development of these reports. Finally, each group was presented with projections of the impact of the program on their business over five years based upon the first year's success. The database marketing manager and sales promotion coordinators then met separately with each brand group to present how to map out an integrated selling program using the database as a resource.

The result was that all brand groups agreed to participate for a three-year period and provide funding for the database. Each felt a sense of ownership of the database, involvement in the program, and a responsibility for feeding the database with new data. The database was a flat file management structure updated on a quarterly basis. Output primarily consisted of hard-copy reports, counts, list pulls, and data extracts for analysis.

A Multistore Test by a Major Retailer

The retailer considering entering data-driven marketing applications operates over 1,000 branch locations across the United States. The organization is the dominant chain in its consumer category. It could successfully rely on mass advertising and word of mouth to generate store traffic, as it is known as the best place to purchase certain products. However, the chain's business is very seasonal, with over 60 percent of chain-wide sales coming during a few key times of the year. Customers are viewed as aggregate statistics purchasing products within certain product departments and categories.

A shift in senior management created an opportunity to introduce data-driven marketing as a tool for customer relationship development. The retailer assigned a team of managers to review external and internal capabilities for development and management of a marketing database and develop a plan to enter data-driven marketing. The team decided that the chain lacked the technical and marketing resources to develop and proceed with such a program. They sought a vendor partner that would conduct a test of data management and marketing to help the team determine if their company should initiate data-driven marketing. Once chosen, the vendor and the management team developed a test plan that included capture at point of sale of all customers, model development identifying high-potential customer segments and prospects, and a communications program with a tracking mechanism.

The test program involved capture of customer telephone numbers at point of sale in over 100 branches for all sales. Each phone number was then reverse-appended to capture the corresponding name and address information. Customer records were then developed over a six-month test period, tracking customers by purchase, frequency of purchase, and some household-level demographics. This process was a large undertaking, given that each store accounted for thousands of sales per day with many data codes associated with each sale. In addition to facilitating cost-effective communications, the test allowed the vendor and retailer to learn the appropriate level of data to capture and how to effectively manage large amounts of sales data.

After three months of data gathering, model and segmentation analysis took place. The goal of the process was first to identify best customers by sales category and department, then to identify high-potential customers by matching them to best customers and high-potential noncustomers located in the participating stores' local market areas. Once identified, communications programs were designed to increase sales based upon relationship, reward, and sales promotion. The communications were designed to get customers to buy outside of their original buying patterns to increase cross-sales, up-sales, and peripheral sales. The results of the communications phase were very successful. Sales increased significantly from the relationship and reward programs. The targeted prospecting programs also were successful compared to previous nontargeted local marketing programs. Results were tracked against two control groups: a segment tracked in the database and a group of stores matching the test program profiles but not included in the program.

The test provided management the necessary information to proceed to implementation of a roll-out program throughout the United States. The database is managed at the vendor location using a relational database management software program on the mainframe. No on-line access tools are associated with the database. Management relies on hard-copy reports, data extracts downloaded for analysis on PCs, and tapes delivered to the modeling and analysis resource. Model scores and behavioral clusters are updated on each customer record on a quarterly basis and all files are updated monthly.

Building a Prototype for an Insurance Marketer

This example involves one of the most successful insurance companies in the United States, a provider of auto, life, and home insurance for millions of Americans. It had worked under the principle of "if it's not broken, don't fix it." The current database worked well for billing, claim tracking, and actuarial accounting. However, it hardly functioned as a marketing resource. The sophisticated marketing team found it nearly impossible to get the information required to model, cross-sell, upgrade, develop new products, or prospect. Thus, a decision was made to determine if using an outside resource for marketing information management would provide marketing benefit and be cost-effective for the company.

The organization created a management team of technical, marketing, and outside consulting resources to evaluate potential outside data management vendors. The chosen vendor was instructed to build a prototype version of a roll-out database. A subset of data representative of the entire business was loaded into the database. All programs that were considered for the roll-out database were tested with the prototype database. Thus, all operational, financial, and marketing programs were evaluated as though a full database were in place.

At the end of a two-year test period, the management committee determined that the prototype system provided significant marketing value in terms of customer upgrade, cross-sell, and product development opportunities and that the cost of a side-by-side external system was justified. The insurance company's total data files were then loaded into the system for roll-out of all marketing programs.

The database was a relational, on-line access program tracking customer behavior and predicting future behavior via customer-generated data and data enhancement. Over 20 modelers access database subsets or extracts on a daily basis. The user-friendly programs provide nontechnical professionals with access to the data for the first time. The insurance company estimated that the new database program increased marketing productivity by over 40 percent and contributed significantly to a 15 percent sales increase in the first roll-out year.

Many variations of the previous themes of selling database to management are possible. You must move forward at a pace that makes sense for your own organization. The key to this process is to examine your organization. You must have or become a champion for data-driven marketing. Then you can create an appropriate plan for selling a database to your management. Many organizations are convinced without a test. Many must see the value of the database demonstrated. Each type of organization can be convinced if you learn an effective way to sell database and develop an appropriate structure to accomplish it.

P A R T

Staying Ahead of the Curve: Future Issues in Database Marketing

A Pattern for the Future: The Database as a Strategic Resource and Customer Contact Marketing

With enough computing power, you've got a marketing department in a box.

Kevin J. Clancy and Robert S. Shulman,
The Marketing Revolution

A marketing department in a box? We hope not! At least not as long as we are doing marketing. However, the statement is not far from the truth. Your marketing database can provide you with the ultimate strategic resource to guide your business.

To develop a database as a strategic resource, you must ask the question, What value does database marketing have for my business? The answer depends on your business. It depends on your organization's marketing applications and the functional integration of your marketing-related activities. You must examine how your organization's business functions relate to marketing and a marketing database. Figure 14-1 is an example of a traditional business structure and its link to a marketing database.

Figure 14-1   Traditional Business Structure and Its Link to a Marketing Database

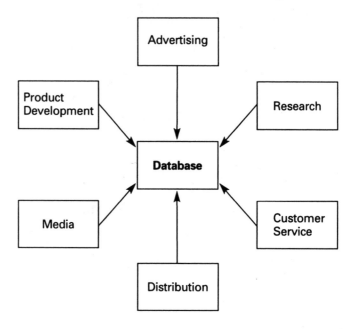

Figure 14-2 represents an integrated business structure and its link to a marketing database. In either situation, the functions that relate to the database must be able to have a give-and-take with the database. There must be a free flow of information back and forth into the database. If your organizational functions are open to change, then development of a strategic database system will be relatively easy. If your business functions are "corporate silos" that resist change and build walls around their areas of function, then development of a strategic database resource will require intervention and coordination at a level above the business functions.

Using a Database to Support Your Strategic Objectives

Generally, a strategic database resource will support a marketer's strategic objectives in the following four areas: gaining competitive advantage, research and product development, business planning, and integrating the marketing communications process.

Figure 14-2   An Integrated Business Structure and Its Link to a Marketing Database

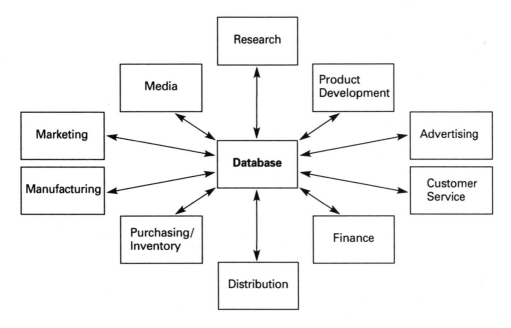

Gaining Competitive Advantage

If your goal is to track your competition, blunt their strategy, and take away their customers, you must set up your database to accomplish this. Your source data strategy must be to identify and capture as much information as you can on your target audience, whether they are customers or not. Over time, you can identify most of your target audience, their relationship with your products or services, and their relationship with your competitors' products and services. This will allow you to counter your competitors' sales offers and convert their customers and keep them loyal to your products and services.

Research and Product Development

Your marketing database can support your research objectives. You can use it as a tool to understand your customers and prospects and their buying behavior. With this knowledge, you can predict future behavior. By understanding customer relationships to existing products and services, leading-edge database marketers can use their database as tools to predict or test new product development. Database-driven testing is much less expensive than market tests and often proves more effective as results are projectable over the entire target audience. A database can also be used to research and test new distribution channels for existing or new products and services.

Business Planning

A database can become your ultimate business planning tool. It can give you an understanding of business requirements including your target audience, media effectiveness, product dynamics, sales process dynamics, distribution process, price dynamics, evaluation of offers, analysis of competitors' sales, products, and customers, and research and development issues. Once you understand your business dynamics, the database can assist you to plot future strategy and trends based upon your knowledge of current and past activity.

Integrating the Marketing Communications Process

Your marketing database can allow you to integrate communications alternatives with the appropriate message and sales opportunity. This is accomplished by developing a system integrating message alternatives, media options, and targeted customer groups (see Figure 14-3).

Figure 14-3   Integrated Marketing Communications Mix

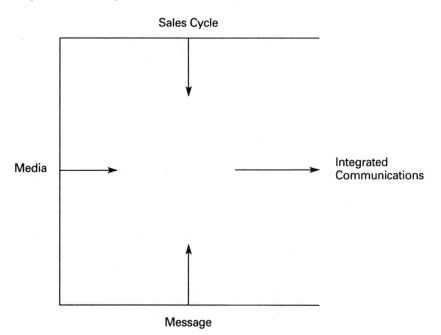

Customer Contact Marketing and the Ultimate Strategic Marketing Database

The ultimate strategic marketing database will be similar to "marketing in a box." It will allow a marketer to access customer and competitive data for decision making. It will allow access to data for achievement of the marketer's strategic objectives. However, the most important use of this database will be as a customer communications management resource.

Reaching a New Level of Customer Communications

The efforts of some database marketers have provided the momentum for a fundamental change in the use of a database as a communications management tool. In fact, this change may ultimately lead data-driven marketing communicators to a new level of communications—*customer contact marketing.*

Similar to direct marketing's evolution from direct mail marketing to direct response marketing to today's direct marketing, database marketing has evolved as well. The first major application-driven technique for database marketing was multimedia direct marketing, in which the computer captured all lead and sales activity over a variety of media. Then came segmented or targeted marketing, in which the database was used to predict consumer response and behavior. Now, customer contact marketing is based upon true relationship-generated marketing communications programs focused on message relevance and customer receptivity. Becoming a customer contact marketer will require some new thinking for some marketers. However, customer contact marketing may ultimately become the standard for marketing communications.

Three Principles of Customer Contact Marketing

Customer contact marketing has three fundamental principles. The first principle is, View the customer as your primary asset. The second is, Create an "outside-in" marketing philosophy. The third is, Manage the communications process.

View the Customer as Your Primary Asset

The customer is your primary asset—not your products or services. While this is not a surprise to many traditional direct marketers, it is new thinking for most marketing organizations. Most marketers, including many direct marketers, view existing and new products and services as their primary assets. Customers mean little more than share of market or numbers of products sold. Customer contact marketers measure the long-term value of a relationship with the customer—whether they sell to 50 individuals or to 40 million households.

Create an "Outside-In" Marketing Philosophy

A marketing database provides customer contact marketers a resource to reinvent their marketing philosophy from "inside-out" to "outside-in" thinking. Inside-out thinking and most traditional marketing and communications programs talk *at* the customer rather than *to* him or her. When products are seen as the asset, inside-out thinking forces the marketer to communicate a universal sales message. Outside-in thinking, on the other hand, forces marketers to understand what the customer wants to know in order to make an initial and repeat purchases and how to best deliver that communication.

Manage the Communications Process

A database provides the customer contact marketer the opportunity to manage all customer contact no matter what media is chosen. All the possible ways to reach your customers must be viewed based on relevance and not on frequency or audience coverage. A database allows you to manage and measure all customer contact media and adjust your message and media accordingly.

The Process of Customer Contact Marketing

Dr. Don Schultz, professor of integrated marketing communications at Northwestern University's Medill School of Journalism, may be the father of customer contact marketing. At the very least, he is the leading speaker on this subject. Schultz calls it integrated marketing communications, but the message is the same. Schultz offered us the following comments: "Technology has killed the mass market. With many nontraditional marketers developing databases, the more they know about their customers, the less they need rely on mass advertising communications." He further states, "The more consumers knows about your product, the less they need traditional advertising." Schultz believes that data-driven marketers of the future must look about the marketplace in a new way by thinking about customers, not products. He suggests the focus should be "How do I create communications programs that are valuable to the customer, and thus valuable to my products or services?"

The basis of customer contact marketing is to view a database as a strategic resource rather than just a tactical one. The database becomes the repository of all we know about our customers that is relevant to facilitating their decision to buy and keep buying our product or service. This includes what information they need to make a decision, what incentive they require to keep buying, and how we should best communicate with the customer to keep an ongoing relationship of providing the right product to meet the customer's needs and wants. Schultz suggests that this is "in-bound versus out-bound" communications strategy. The traditional way to view marketing communications is to view communications programs as support for the sales process—an "out-bound" strategy. The new perspective of customer contact marketers is that communications leads the sales effort, which is an "in-bound" communications strategy.

Once you have made a commitment to develop a database as an in-bound communications resource, you must stock it with the right kinds of data to make informed communications decisions. This means behavior-based data—data that comes from actual consumer purchases, not information on what people intend to purchase. In addition, you will want to gather data on why they purchase, how frequently they purchase, and what other products they purchase. Beyond behavior-based data, relevant demographics that describe the household, such as age ranges, sex, marital status, income ranges, and family composition will be valuable.

With the correct information in your database, customer contact marketing is a four-step process requiring customer classification analysis, media receptivity identification, message relevance, and contact management.

Step 1: Customer Classification Analysis

The first step in the customer contact marketing process is to classify your customers based upon their purchasing relationship with your products and services. A consumer products example of this classification system might contain the following four categories: purchasers of competitive products, trial purchasers, infrequent purchasers of our product, and brand-loyal customers.

Figure 14-4   Consumer Product Example

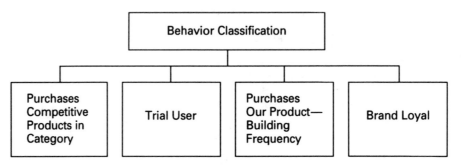

It is more realistic that a typical consumer products model might have seven, ten, or even more classifications. A financial services example might include the following classifications:

Figure 14-5   Financial Services Example

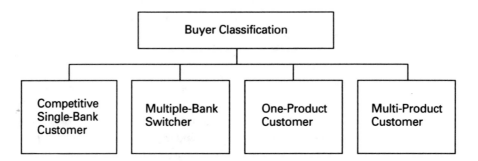

For large consumer products databases, which can have as many as 30 or 40 million records, the process of relationship marketing does not mean a unique communications program for each and every household. By logically grouping customers and prospects by their behavior-based classifications, you can focus the same message to a larger group of customers based upon similar purchase behavior.

Step 2: Media Receptivity Identification

Once customers are classified by behavior, the customer contact marketer must choose among the array of communications options that can deliver a relevant message to the customer. The options include all possible contact points a customer has with your product and service. Some consumer products media options might include:

- National or local television
- Cable
- Radio
- Newspapers
- Magazines
- Co-ops
- FSIs
- Point-of-purchase
- In-store display
- Direct mail
- Outbound telemarketing
- 800 numbers
- Event marketing
- On-package
- Third party promotions

Communications options must be evaluated by their ability to deliver a message based upon the product information requirements of the particular customer classification. This evaluation is accomplished by comparing targeting capability, cost, and consumer receptivity to the media. It is likely that several message delivery options will be used in combination to effectively communicate with customer groups.

Step 3: Message Relevance

With the first two steps completed, the correct communication can be crafted to facilitate the consumers' needs in relation to your product or service. The array of message options can include image or equity advertising communications, promotion, detailed information, relationship communications, customer service, and personal consultation.

Step 4: Contact Management

Once the consumer has been classified and the correct media and message identified, the ongoing customer contact marketing programs are developed. The process can be visualized in three dimensions as in Figure 14-3. Given our knowledge of our customer at any point in time in relation to the purchase of our products and services, we can modify the combination of media and message accordingly.

The process of customer communications management and contact is illustrated in Figure 14-6. In this three-sided matrix, the top represents the consumer's purchase decision and your company. For example, in the consumer products example shown, the customer could have one of six purchase decision relationships with your product. These include:

- **Not in category.** Consumer does not currently purchase products in your category. For example, the family does not use automatic dishwasher detergent

- **In category.** Consumer purchases in the category, but not your brand

- **Trial user.** Consumer purchases your brand one time

- **Frequency user.** Consumer has purchased your brand on a periodic basis

- **Switcher.** Consumer switches back and forth among a number of brands

- **Loyal.** Consumer is loyal to your brand

Over time, with a concentrated source data strategy, the customer contact marketer would attempt to group all database households and/or the entire target audience in a database by the above categorizations.

Contact method is shown on the left side of the matrix in Figure 14-6. Contact method represents all available media options ranked in order of their ability to facilitate the unique consumer information requirements of each consumer group in the sales cycle. Each consumer group may have a different combination of communications techniques applied based upon their relationship with the product.

At the bottom of the matrix in Figure 14-6 is message management. Each message designed to meet the appropriate consumer information requirement is matched to media and target audience group. The three types of messages for the consumer products example are awareness or brand image, promotion, and relationship building or reinforcement.

Figure 14-6   Customer Communications Contact Matrix

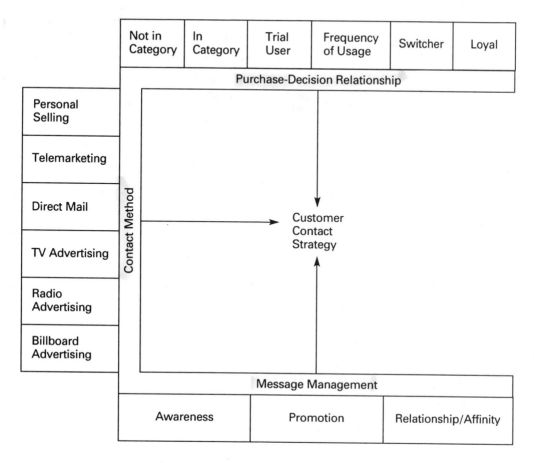

Over time, the customer contact marketer can measure customer performance or purchase behavior based upon the customer's income stream. This creates a lifetime value model for each customer classification. The model's projected payout will determine the communications expenditures' level baseline. For example, the marketer calculates the income stream and net profit of a customer in the loyal group, which will determine the contribution of that customer to communications efforts. Communications to elicit initial trial and repurchase by a customer will usually cost more than ongoing communications. This is due to promotional costs and multiple contacts to facilitate purchase of a specific product over another. These communications usually include both targeted media, such as direct mail, and untargeted media, such as network television. As a customer becomes loyal, the communications will tend to be more targeted (relational or direct mail for example) than untargeted. Even though targeted media is usually more expensive on a per-contact basis, the value of the relationship measured in frequency of purchase and income stream will more than offset increased communications costs. In fact, the marketer will realize increased profits per customer because the most expensive per-contact media are focused on the best customers.

Each customer group requires different information to purchase and repurchase your product. Different groups will require or use different combinations of media to fulfill this requirement. For example, the group "switchers" may break down into five or ten subgroups determined by characteristics other than product purchase. Usually, demographics and lifestyle indicators will determine subcharacteristics. Some examples of subcharacteristics might be households of two singles, one adult and one child, empty nesters, two adults and one small child, and two adults and three children of various ages. All of these examples could require different communications options for households in the same product groups. For example, two adults with no children and two adults with three children may buy the same product for different reasons. The customer contact must recognize this in order to facilitate the appropriate information search.

With a value model in place on each customer classification and subclassification, the marketer can match targeted and untargeted media with appropriate messages to deliver a managed customer contact program. Each customer contact is registered in the customer record on the database. Contacts are accumulated and reconciled against the model. This allows for constant revalidation of the model and the projected payout.

What Customer Contact Marketing Requires . . . and Offers

Creating a database system to manage customer contact marketing goes back to the foundation of the three key building blocks, data, technology, and statistical techniques. In this case, the process could be quite simple. Customer contact marketing does not require on-line, relational database technology. It does require enough storage capability to manage sufficient data about your customers to make informed long-term decisions. The research techniques are also not formidable. Consumers will tend to segment themselves by their purchase activity. Determination of subsegments will require analytical techniques to understand purchase patterns by lifestyle or socioeconomic groupings.

The major expense and effort of a customer contact program is in source data strategy. The marketer must invest time and money to stock the database with behavioral and demographic data. Most information requirements of a customer contact database can be handled with hard-copy reports. Additional expenses will be incurred if management wants to access and compare customer data on-line.

Customer contact marketing represents both a new way of thinking for many marketers and a way to survive in the post mass-marketing world. It offers a methodology that facilitates customer-based communications and creates long-term customer relationships. By allowing the marketer to control media and message options, it increases message relevance by reaching a receptive consumer. Customer contact marketing may well be the ultimate example of database marketing and the future for database-driven communications and consumer marketing as well.

Social Issues in Database Marketing: Environmental Waste and Consumer Privacy

As direct marketers, we are currently facing the biggest challenge in our industry's history. A challenge that is a direct result of our phenomenal success.

Jerome W. Pickholz, chairman and CEO, Ogilvy & Mather Direct,
A Call to Action for America's Direct Marketers (Ogilvy & Mather, 1992)

Two major social issues face database marketers today: environmental waste and consumer privacy. These issues are a direct result of our industry's visibility and growth. They are so important to the future of data-driven communications that we feel we must take a stand on them . . . and attempt to make you a believer too.

We live in a world that will not let us shelter ourselves and our businesses from outside influences. With instant mass media coverage of issues and political posturing for electorates, legitimate consumer concerns are often blown out of proportion. While this chapter will focus on privacy, we feel that it is important to also mention environmental concerns and how direct mail usage has been distorted for sensational coverage.

Environmental Waste and Direct Mail Usage

In 1988, the nation tossed out 180 million tons of garbage, according to the Environmental Protection Agency. That same year, the Postal Service processed 3.8 million tons of third class mail. If every piece of that mail found its way to the landfill, third class mail would have represented only 2 percent of the nation's trash production for 1988. By contrast, newspapers and other paper products account for nearly 40 percent of the nation's garbage. Even if the direct mail contribution is 4 percent today, the paradox is that newspapers, magazines, and books cast stones at direct mail and not at themselves as environmental abusers.

This is not to say that direct mail users are not contributors to the problem of environmental waste. And we must do our share to solve this problem. Through the use of recycled paper and water-soluble inks, we can become leaders in environmental responsibility. We can do it by choice, because we are citizens of the planet, or we can be forced to do it by legislation sometime in the future and continue to be unfairly maligned by larger polluters looking for an easy target to blame. It's our choice, as an industry and as individuals.

Recycling and environmental concern does not, by the way, end with direct mail for our businesses. An environmentally concerned organization also recycles paper, is concerned about air pollution, supports local community efforts, car pooling, and many other issues.

Privacy and the Database Marketer

As individuals, direct marketers are generally sensitive to the issue of privacy. Privacy is part of our basic freedom as citizens of the United States. We as a single voice do not wish to see George Orwell's version of the future. Yet, in our role as database marketers, privacy represents the single most important issue facing our industry.

Many responsible consumers that feel that we, as information-based marketers, have already created a form of Orwellian future. A TRW newsletter paints the following disturbing picture of privacy and a hypothetical American family: "A divorced mother of two children is facing her birthday next month. Her roof leaks, her house needs painting, and she has not had a vacation in two years. She worries about her future. With today's mail, she hits the boiling point. In it are a few bills, a realtor's flyer, a catalog, a learning center announcement, a contribution request, coupons for service at the local car dealership, and a contractor's offer to add another bedroom to her home. She opens one of the envelopes. Happy Birthday, it begins. . . . She rages that 'they' know it is her birthday, that she owns her home, that she has kids . . . etc." TRW goes on to speculate that this woman has just become America's newest privacy advocate.

Jerry W. Pickholz, chairman and CEO of Ogilvy & Mather Direct, penned a pamphlet called "A Call to Action for America's Direct Marketers" (Ogilvy & Mather, 1992). In it he states, "Suddenly, the very tools that help us perform our jobs better . . . exacerbate the concerns of citizens who wonder: Just how much do they know about me? And who are they selling that information to?" Privacy is an issue that affects every database marketer.

Database marketers have an enormous responsibility related to the privacy issue and must be the leaders in making the negative focus of this issue a positive one. After all, customers are our business. It is not in our interest that consumers view us as Big Brother. We want them to understand that by knowing our customers, we can more efficiently meet their needs. . . . But consumers are not getting the message!

The core of the problem is in our communications to customers or prospects. Our primary tools for delivering these communications are direct mail and telemarketing. Telemarketing is perceived as abused by many politicians and consumers. In fact, we as consumers object to many of the calls we receive each night up to and past 9:30 p.m. The widespread abuse is perceived so intensely that it is hard to count the number of telemarketing-related pieces of legislation that are on the docket across the United States.

The medical profession differentiates between symptoms and cause in diagnosing a problem. The perceived threat to privacy is not a cause in this case. It is a symptom. The cause of our problem is a lack of responsibility by many data-driven marketers to understand and address legitimate consumer privacy concerns.

Your Marketing Database and Confidentiality of Information

In order to be responsible as a database marketer in the area of consumer privacy, you must clearly understand the issues and how they impact your database and your marketing efforts. The two key aspects of the privacy issue that affect database marketers are confidentiality of information and the right to privacy.

Confidentiality of Information: Internal Use of Data

The concept of confidentiality of information breaks down into categories of use of customer information. The first is the use of data about a customer for the company's own internal marketing efforts. This implies that a marketer gathers or purchases data on customers to target customer marketing programs. Consumers seem to be split on this use of data. If an offer is particularly relevant to them, they are more interested in hearing about it from the marketer. However, they remain concerned about the extent of the information that the marketer keeps about them. We feel that consumers believe database marketers have significantly more information about them in their databases than they actually do. This is due to sensationalized media coverage of this issue. The solution to this problem has three parts: honesty, responsible use of customer data, and responsible communications with noncustomers.

Figure 15-1

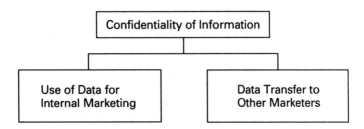

Be Honest with Your Customers

Tell them what information you keep in your database that relates to them. Once they understand how limited the data is, they probably will not be concerned. If a few customers object to the level of data you maintain, you can be proactive by eliminating this information from their records and thus eliminating a problem for your customer.

Be Responsible in the Customer Relationship

If you have created a dialog with your customers or prospects to gain a particular type of data, then simply be responsible with how you use what you know. For example, if the customer told you his or her birth-date, then it is all right to acknowledge that birth-date. If your customer purchased a product from you, it is all right to communicate and acknowledge this fact.

Be Responsible in Non-customer Communications

If you have gathered a particular piece of data via a source data strategy other than customer dialog, then you must communicate based upon your knowledge without specifically referring to the data.

Confidentiality of Information: Selling Data

The second issue in confidentiality of information is selling data that you have gathered about the customer to a third party. The transfer of information could be as simple as a barter of lists of last year's catalog buyers or of various demographic characteristics such as name, children's data, or income. As a responsible marketer, if you collect information from your customers, ask them if it is all right to share this data, or if they want to receive offers from other organizations targeted to their interests. I recently added a code to my name when subscribing to a new media video magazine. I began to see the coded name show up on the most unbelievable types of communications. Recently it showed up in my mailbox on a solicitation for a charity ball before the 1993 Auto Show. How my name got from a new media video magazine to an Auto Show benefit is beyond me. In any case, this was an unprofessional use of list transfer and an untargeted communications effort that resulted in a waste of money and, worse, could result in cynical consumers.

In the future, database marketers who sell or barter information are going to have to assume responsibility for the propriety of transferring this data to another marketer. This translates to managing the sensitivity of the data and the relevance of the potential communications that will be delivered to the consumer.

Database Marketing and the Right to Privacy

The second major privacy issue is the right to privacy. We as database marketers must accept that some consumers simply do not want to receive direct mail. They view this as a civil liberty issue, suggesting that unsolicitated mail is an invasion of their person.

Figure 15-2

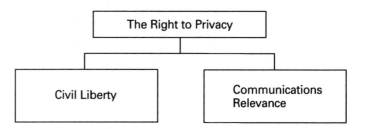

If consumers feel this way, we must comply. We as an industry must allow and help consumers to opt out of direct mail and telemarketing communications if they do not want to receive them, before the government does it for us.

The second part of the right to privacy is relevance. A growing body of research suggests that consumers who have opted out of all direct mail or telemarketing eventually reconsider the decision. They really were trying to increase the relevance of the mail and telemarketing they received, not to cut themselves off from all direct advertising communications.

So, where do we go from here? We as database marketers must empower the consumer!

Part of the answer is to change our thinking process. In the seventies and eighties, our thinking process was, "How can I reach my customers?" In the nineties, as database marketers our approach must be, "How can my customers reach me?" This approach will encourage a dialog with customers that will provide a device to encourage feedback on how successful we are in our effort to gain a common understanding of how we use information. We look at this process as outside-in rather than inside-out thinking.

We must create a real dialog with consumers. We can only do this by listening more and talking less. We must develop a mechanism within our data-driven marketing programs to facilitate our ability to listen to consumer concerns and interests. Several marketers are already leading the way. One major database marketer routinely asks customers to tell them the best time and way to contact them. Should they call or write or send a fax? At what time? At home or work? The marketer then works hard to make sure that all communications are within the customers' request parameters. This dialog lets the customer participate in the communications process and allows the marketer to find a relevant way to communicate with the customer.

Just as you have a board of directors in your business, create a consumer advisory board. Empower this board to advise you on how to be sensitive to your customers' privacy and other customer service concerns. Then merchandise the power of this process to all customers. Let them know that a panel of their peers is looking over your shoulder to see that all the data you capture and maintain is used only for the right purposes. Let them know that this group has approved a policy for trade, barter, or sale of data based upon their understanding of your business and consumers' privacy concerns.

Begin to think of your customer as a gatekeeper. In the future, only relevant communications are going to be let into the gate. You as a marketer must help make the process of guarding the gate easier for the consumer or he or she will stop letting advertising communications in. A sociological theory known as *uncertainty absorption* is now being reviewed by academic direct marketers. The foundation of uncertainty absorption theory is that individuals hate uncertainty and have only a limited ability to handle it. The application of the theory for database marketing and privacy is that by taking away the uncertainty by increasing message relevance, we overcome the consumer's objection to receiving marketing communications.

We must demonstrate to U.S. consumers and their representatives that we are ready to work with them to increase the relevance of our communications. We can accomplish this through several activities. First, we must create a dialog with customers. Second, we must encourage ongoing industry-sponsored efforts to identify and comply with consumers who want to act as gatekeepers of their mail and telephone communications. Third, we must devote great study to understand and develop proactive solutions to consumer concerns.

Some Final Words on Privacy

Database marketers must assume responsibility for the privacy issue and turn it from a threat to an opportunity. If we view privacy as a threat, we will develop only a defense and spend money only to lobby against regulation. As an opportunity, we can be creative and develop a proactive way to deal with this issue. We can do this by investing in devices that will show our customers that we are sensitive and concerned about their privacy concerns, and by educating database marketers on the proactive measures they can implement. We must link the bottom line of the privacy issue to each marketer's bottom line. (The Direct Marketing Association, representing the direct marketing and database marketing community, has taken a leadership position on privacy. For more information, contact the DMA in New York or the Chicago Association of Direct Marketing in Chicago.)

We can empower consumers to be the gatekeepers of all information we send them through the mail or over the telephone. We can accomplish this with consumer dialog, uncertainty absorption, and a sensitivity to what information we gather and how we use it.

C H A P T E R 16

Future Trends in Database Marketing

The only thing that is certain about the future is that people keep trying to predict it.

Jackson and Wang and every other would-be predictor

Writers and futuristic thinkers are looking to the new millennium. Incredible changes have occurred in our world over the past 1,000 years. In fact, there have been unbelievable changes in just the last 100 years . . . 50 years, even the last 20 years. One change we can agree about is that the pace of new technological development is increasing rapidly.

Sit back and ponder for a moment the pace and types of change over the next 20 or 50 years. There is no question that some of it will relate directly to database marketing. This change will affect the key building blocks of database marketing and the marketing environment in which we operate and communicate.

A New Generation of Consumers

Top on any list of change for communicators is our target, the consumer. We can argue for or against major change in consumer lifestyle and purchasing behavior. It is reasonable to speculate that leisure time will continue to become more precious. Consumers will desire to spend less time making routine decisions, put more order in their lives, and enjoy them more. We doubt that in our lifetime consumers will be willing to give up face-to-face shopping as their primary purchase channel. However, alternative purchase channels such as catalogs and home shopping will continue to grow at a faster pace than traditional retail sales. Consumers will choose purchasing channels and alternatives that offer them the ability to maximize the shopping experience in a minimum time. As the population ages, product and service demands will change, and future retailers must react accordingly.

The most interesting phenomenon is in our new generation of consumers. Rob Jackson did not touch a computer until he was almost 30. His 3-year-old son is already playing computer games with him. He will master the computer in grade school. Modems, faxes, on-line computer access, and most important, the integration of all communications tools will be commonplace by the time he reaches his purchasing power potential. Just think of the potential and dynamics of the change represented by my son's generation.

We must examine and prepare for two different consumers in the next 20 years. The first is the traditional consumer raised in today's world who is adapting his or her purchase behavior patterns as our world changes. To reach this group, we can adapt our existing techniques of data-driven marketing to understand their needs and wants and communications requirements. The second is a new generation of consumers that has grown up with technology and the lifestyle changes implemented by the traditional group. None of the traditional rules will apply. We can only speculate on how to communicate with and sell to this new frontier of consumers.

To look at where data-driven marketing is going between now, the year 2000, and beyond, let us look at five important ingredients of data-driven marketing, including the three building blocks plus two more:

- Technology
- Data
- Research
- Communications
- Business decisions

Technology: Increases in Accessibility and Ease of Use

It is clear that the trend toward pushing information usage down to the lowest possible level of technology will continue. Today's market leaders are already seeing the writing on the wall. Traditional mainframe business is and will move in a downward sales spiral. Even IBM has admitted that the future is in massively parallel processing, distributed processing, and RISC technology, and not in the large processors they are currently producing.

With data storage and data processing power increasing in capacity at progressively lower costs, managing and manipulating even the largest customer databases is no longer difficult. PC power is the future. PCs linked to workstations, minicomputers, and mainframes via client servers are quickly becoming the rule. So many exciting new technologies are on the horizon that they are hard to keep up with. Some include:

- New flash memory storage technology
- Data storage in matchbox-size space
- Wireless PC links connecting PCs and fax modems together without telephone lines
- Palm-size information processors with the ability to handle more information than current PCs, which will interact with stored databases anywhere and at any time with user-friendly access software and interfaces
- Network technology linking unlimited numbers and types of PCs together in local and national networks

It is safe to say that hardware and software combinations will allow managers of the future to access any level of database marketing information on their PCs in the office, by the pool, or on the airplane, manipulate that information, and present it in graphic and word processing formats. It's here today, to some extent.

Few truly user-friendly data access structures exist today. Resources like MarketPulse or Cross/Z International are prototypes. End users will be able to access any combination of marketing-related data in point-and-click format for analysis, communications programs, and management information. Business decisions will be made with a new level of capability. We also anticipate that research and analytical tools will be built into the new data management and data access tools, allowing managers to create models and score a database on the fly.

Data: More Information Will Allow More Relevant Communications

As we have discussed in Chapter 15, the continued use of consumer information will depend on responsibility in the gathering, management, and use of the data. Without this responsibility, database marketing will have a limited future.

We see three basic types of consumer information converging to provide database marketers with a true customer picture for targeting purposes. This information will include relevant demographics at the household and individual levels, leisure interest data illustrating a consumer's nonworking activity, and propensity and product purchase data. As processing power increases and data storage becomes less expensive, more and more point-of-purchase data will be tracked to the consumer and become available for targeting programs. We see a trend toward development of a new source data strategy especially for nontraditional database marketers—survey data to identify large numbers of users and competitive users as well as point-of-sale data for all customers in the retail environment.

The convergence of these three dimensions of consumer information will provide database marketers of the future the ability to target by any combination of consumer characteristics via sophisticated analytical and modeling technology. In the future, there will be no excuse for not understanding your customers' or prospects' purchase behavior propensity and no reason to waste communications costs by communicating to an uninterested audience.

Research: User-Friendly Modeling and Learning Systems

We believe that modeling and statistical analysis techniques will become more and more integrated into data access. This trend is driven by more and more PC access to information. In the future, simple model and segmentation systems will be conducted in a user-friendly environment as a part of the count and analysis functions performed by marketers. For example, a marketer will identify in the database a count or extract of a customer segment with customer characteristics attached such as best customers and their demographics and purchasing behavior. The computer will translate this to a model and score the database immediately to identify look-alike customers. This analysis now is accomplished off-line by research professionals. In the future, a marketer will initiate and execute the model and have results in minutes. Complex analytical problems, however, will still be handled by researchers off line.

We feel that modeling techniques will lose much of the black-box mystique. New techniques such as the Fractal Navigator from Cross/Z and Donnelley Marketing's Multi-Model provide researchers and marketers alike with easy-to-understand views of the data behind the models and compare multiple techniques so the marketer can pick the technique that produces the best results.

One of the exciting new areas for the future is learning systems such as neuronetworks. These systems are able to "learn" from results, becoming "smart" in predicting results and behavior. Research tools that increase the accuracy of their prediction power with data experience will ultimately provide new levels of capabilities for database marketers.

Communications: Individualized Messages

Communications is the area that potentially will see the most change over the next 10 to 20 years. As we have stated, the end of using the mass market for all communications efforts is at hand. The consumer wants relevant information to facilitate the purchase of products and services. The future of all communications programs is inevitably intertwined with data and data-driven marketing. Consumers want relevant information and databases allow marketers to understand what they need and to deliver relevant information.

We see that this process may at some point lead to one-on-one marketing or household marketing for even the largest marketers. Envision, please, the year 2060. Each individual has a telephone number that follows him or her for life, no matter where he or she lives. In addition, each household has a communications center that integrates telecommunications, video communications, and data communications. Now, enter the Universal Computer Products Company, which after several mergers has over 500 products representing over 85 fast-moving consumer product categories in the United States and the world. Universal has a database of over 140 million households. The database contains customer demographics and purchase behavior on all Universal and category purchases by each household. This database was initiated in 2034, when all major fast-moving products retailers coordinated their data collection into one massive database due to the cost and data volume associated with individual data collection.

Universal is able to create 25 versions of each product commercial representing the major customer groupings for the product. Inside each commercial is a 30-second space for a custom communication that is delivered to each household uniquely via the database and lifetime consumer telephone number. The custom message acknowledges the purchase the customer made last month or week and recommends repurchase based on history or provides a loyalty incentive based on frequency of purchase. Universal has accomplished a targeted information facilitation for product purchase and a unique direct communication targeted to each purchaser of the product.

You may doubt it will happen. But we believe it will and, in fact, that it is inevitable given the vision, technology, data, and research techniques we can see emerging today. The true power of database marketing communications is in our children's young hands today.

Business Decisions Will Be Driven by Database Marketing

Business decisions and management information of the future will be raised to a level never thought possible by data-driven marketing. Just think about the possibilities. With sophisticated tools to track all product purchases, promotions, communications, and production and distribution costs and relate them back to the individual consumer and then aggregate the data upward in any combination, business decision making will really become a science. Management can, on any time frame they choose, review product cost by sale, product mix by sale, or affect and implication of communications and promotion, and effectively change any of these. Business planning will become a function driven and monitored by the database marketing effort. For example, a grocery chain can track all products purchased, frequency of purchase, and the communications implication of the purchase (whether the purchase resulted from manufacturer promotion, in-store promotion, or retailer-targeted promotion, for example). With this data, store display space, communications programs, purchase incentives, and even programs aimed at altering customer purchase behavior can be monitored, evaluated, and changed. This process will allow the retailer to understand profitability and margin by product, by consumer, and with promotional implication. It will control ordering, merchandise selection, presentation, promotion, and many other aspects of the retailer's business. Data-driven marketing and a database will become the decision making tool for the future of business decisions.

Some Trends over the Next Few Years

Who's Doing What?

The movement by marketers to database use tends to cross most applications and industries. In general, the greatest opportunity obviously lies in industries where marketing databases are now less frequently used. These industries are characterized by multiple distribution channels and multiple customer communications alternatives. For industries in which database marketing is standard operating procedure, the opportunity lies in upgrading data, technology, and research as business objectives become harder to meet with current systems and resources.

We feel that the following data-driven marketing applications will rank high for development of new and improved databases in the 1990s:

- Business-to-business applications, including business-to-consumer/business-to-business joint distribution
- Consumer products manufacturers
- Retailers
- Financial services
- Franchise or dealer programs
- Publishing
- Third-party programs.

Who's Providing Services?

Generally, organizations providing services for database marketing fall into four categories:

- **Database technical services providers.** Provide technical support but not usually data or research
- **Database marketing services providers.** Provide data, technology, research, consulting, and sometimes creative services
- **Database marketing consulting.** Providers usually have strong analytical skills and provide varying combinations of research, technology, and marketing consulting
- **Advertising agencies providing database marketing services.** These are rare. They generally maintain technical, marketing, research, and data skills on staff as well as creative skills. These agencies usually outsource data management

Over the next several years, the trend toward rapid development of databases will continue. However, with the proliferation of PC systems and packaged products, many systems will not meet the ongoing requirements of users. We suspect that by the end of the 1990s, the rapid development of new systems will end and significantly fewer new systems will be developed. At that point, the focus will be on providing the services to make existing systems functional for marketing applications and upgrading the resources of inadequate systems. The database provider of the next millennium will provide all the elements required to provide true data-driven marketing application solutions.

Our Interactive Future . . .

We are constantly reading about the advent of the Information Super Highway. Large technology, entertainment and communications companies are vying for position. Virtual reality in arcades and theaters is just around the corner. What does this mean for database marketers? First, the reality of interactive communications is still a few years off. Second, we cannot stand around waiting. The development of a chip that will link your telephone, cable network, and a smart controller similar to a computer will allow you dominance over interactive communications. You as a consumer will pick and choose bundles of audio/visual options. One may be for entertainment, another education, another for messages, and yet another for offers from selected marketers. Your control center will monitor more than 500 linked channels and select your custom packages.

Database marketers will be able to integrate customer databases, in-home communications, and cable to provide truly targeted communications of the future. Understanding and experimenting with our interactive future is crucial to the future success of database marketing.

We hope that our look at the future has stimulated your thinking about where database marketing is going over the next 20 to 50 years. The most important point is that change is inevitable . . . and the pace of change is increasing. You must plan for this and keep focused on the key building blocks of database marketing—data, technology, and statistical techniques.

Good luck!

I N D E X

TITLES OF INTEREST IN MARKETING,
DIRECT MARKETING, AND SALES PROMOTION

SUCCESSFUL DIRECT MARKETING METHODS, Fourth Edition, by Bob Stone
PROFITABLE DIRECT MARKETING, Second Edition, by Jim Kobs
CREATIVE STRATEGY IN DIRECT MARKETING, by Susan K. Jones
READINGS AND CASES IN DIRECT MARKETING, by Herb Brown and Bruce Buskirk
STRATEGIC DATABASE MARKETING, by Robert R. Jackson and Paul Wang
SUCCESSFUL TELEMARKETING, Second Edition, by Bob Stone and John Wyman
BUSINESS TO BUSINESS DIRECT MARKETING, by Robert Bly
INTEGRATED MARKETING COMMUNICATIONS, by Don E. Schultz, Stanley I. Tannenbaum, and Robert F.
    Lauterborn
NEW DIRECTIONS IN MARKETING, by Aubrey Wilson
GREEN MARKETING, by Jacquelyn Ottman
MARKETING CORPORATE IMAGE: THE COMPANY AS YOUR NUMBER ONE PRODUCT, by James R. Gregory with
    Jack G. Wiechmann
HOW TO CREATE SUCCESSFUL CATALOGS, by Maxwell Sroge
SALES PROMOTION ESSENTIALS, Second Edition, by Don E. Schultz, William A. Robinson and Lisa Petrison
PROMOTIONAL MARKETING: IDEAS AND TECHNIQUES FOR SUCCESS IN SALES PROMOTION, by William A. Robinson
    and Christine Hauri
BEST SALES PROMOTIONS, Sixth Edition, by William A. Robinson
INSIDE THE LEADING MAIL ORDER HOUSES, Third Edition, by Maxwell Sroge
NEW PRODUCT DEVELOPMENT, Second Edition, by George Gruenwald
NEW PRODUCT DEVELOPMENT CHECKLISTS, by George Gruenwald
CLASSIC FAILURES IN PRODUCT MARKETING, by Donald W. Hendon
THE COMPLETE TRAVEL MARKETING HANDBOOK, by Andrew Vladimir
HOW TO TURN CUSTOMER SERVICE INTO CUSTOMER SALES, by Bernard Katz
THE MARKETING PLAN, by Robert K. Skacel
ADVERTISING & MARKETING CHECKLISTS, by Ron Kaatz
SECRETS OF SUCCESSFUL DIRECT MAIL, by Richard V. Benson
U.S. DEPARTMENT OF COMMERCE GUIDE TO EXPORTING
HOW TO GET PEOPLE TO DO THINGS YOUR WAY, by J. Robert Parkinson
THE 1-DAY MARKETING PLAN, by Roman A. Hiebing, Jr. and Scott W. Cooper
HOW TO WRITE A SUCCESSFUL MARKETING PLAN, by Roman G. Hiebing, Jr. and Scott W. Cooper
DEVELOPING, IMPLEMENTING, AND MANAGING EFFECTIVE MARKETING PLANS, by Hal Goetsch
HOW TO EVALUATE AND IMPROVE YOUR MARKETING DEPARTMENT, by Keith Sparling and Gerard Earls
SELLING TO A SEGMENTED MARKET, by Chester A. Swenson
MARKET-ORIENTED PRICING, by Michael Morris and Gene Morris
STATE-OF-THE-ART MARKETING RESEARCH, by A.B. Blankenship and George E. Breen
WAS THERE A PEPSI GENERATION BEFORE PEPSI DISCOVERED IT?, by Stanley C. Hollander and Richard Germain
BUSINESS TO BUSINESS COMMUNICATIONS HANDBOOK, by Fred Messner
SALES LEADS: HOW TO CONVERT EVERY PROSPECT INTO A CUSTOMER, by Robert Donath, James Obermeyer, Carol
    Dixon and Richard Crocker
AMA MARKETING TOOLBOX (SERIES), by David Parmerlee & Allan Sutherlin
AMA COMPLETE GUIDE TO SMALL BUSINESS MARKETING, by Ken Cook
101 TIPS FOR MORE PROFITABLE CATALOGS, by Maxwell Sroge
HOW TO GET THE MOST OUT OF TRADE SHOWS, by Steve Miller
HOW TO GET THE MOST OUT OF SALES MEETINGS, by James Dance
MARKETING TO CHINA, by Xu Bai Yi
STRATEGIC MARKET PLANNING, by Robert J. Hamper and L. Sue Baugh
COMMONSENSE DIRECT MARKETING, Second Edition, by Drayton Bird
NTC'S DICTIONARY OF DIRECT MAIL AND MAILING LIST TERMINOLOGY AND TECHNIQUES, by Nat G. Bodian

For further information or a current catalog, write:
NTC Business Books
a division of *NTC Publishing Group*
4255 West Touhy Avenue
NTC Lincolnwood, Illinois 60646-1975 U.S.A.